YOUR SHAPING
&
MAKING

The Tests and Trials That Form You

Book # 4 From The "Seasoned For Destiny" Series

Sally Mahihu

Table of Contents

Chapter 1

Processed For Destiny

Trusting The Process Of Your Moulding And Making

Chapter 2

The Storms Of A Destiny Survivor

Weathering The Storms Of Life And Coming Through Stronger

Chapter 3

The Scars Of A Sculptured Woman

Turning Your Scars Into Stars

Chapter 4

The Pain Patterns Of A Destiny Champion

Projecting Your Pain Points Into Power Points

Chapter 5

The Pitstops Of A Destiny Racer

Refueling At Defining Moments In Your Journey

Chapter 6

Principled For Destiny

Adopting The Codes And Habits That Will Guide You To Destiny

Dedication

I dedicate this book to every woman who chooses to embrace the process of her making no matter how painful, because she understands that without that process, she can never become the vessel of destiny she was born to be.

Acknowledgement

First and foremost, I would like to thank God for enabling me to write and finish this Book Series. I pray these books will impact and bless many Women who are determined to fulfil their Destiny.

I would like to thank my **Husband Ngari** who really "gets me" and who I refer to as my "Destiny Spouse" because indeed he is a true gift from God and he has been supportive beyond measure during the course of my writing, these Books, in more ways than I can count.

My **sons Eric and Chris,** who are truly sons of my strength, and who have also supported and encouraged me in my "Destiny endeavours" no matter how radically insane I sounded at times.

My late **Dad, Chris Kahara** who constantly affirmed me and instilled the confidence I needed to embark on many "Destiny journeys" leading to where and who I am today.

Rev Teresa Wairimu, my "Destiny Midwife" who has spoken into my life for the past two decades and who has been diligent in nurturing, moulding and shaping me, to birth out the gifts within me (even during the times when my own foolishness and short-sightedness, coupled with a zeal that was often devoid of knowledge threatened to abort my Purpose and Calling.)

H.E. Madam Rachel Ruto who is equally passionate about the empowerment of women and who I admire and respect tremendously for her continuous and tireless commitment to better the lives of women in our society and Nation.

My Aunt Rev Judy Mbugua for believing in me and for being a pillar of strength to me for over the years as a Mother figure, for teaching me that my roles as a wife and mother are not an excuse for, but rather an incentive to fulfil my Purpose and Destiny.

My friend and Mentor Dr. Herta Von Stigel who came into my life, at just the right time and helped me to understand that I needed to conquer the Mountain within me before I could conquer the Mountains around me, and whose invaluable friendship and mentorship is a great source of encouragement for me.

My diligent research Assistants and Typists **Victor M. Mwangi, Frida Wanjira** and **Tecla Karimi** who all worked tirelessly in making these books happen.

My Publisher & Cover Designer Shadrack Radido of House Of Wealth Publishers who allowed me the freedom I needed in this Series of Books even when I stubbornly chose to deviate from the traditional Book writing ethics and who has been a solid sounding board on the many technical issues regarding this Series.

My Editor Dr. Mark Stibbe for his excellent editing and no-nonsense professional approach, truly a gift in the literary world.

My die-hard Spice Girls and faithful Women from my Seasoned Woman Vision who cheer me on and whose undeterred insistent claims that there is still more in me for them than I let out, warms my heart and provokes me to keep doing that which I was created for.

Everyone else who contributed in one way or another to the conception and birthing of this Series of Books.

Foreword

I have known Sally for over two decades now from the time she joined and begun to serve me in Ministry. Sally is a very zealous and passionate Woman in whatever she believes in.

Beyond her professional career as a Lawyer, Sally has demonstrated strong gifts of speaking, teaching, mentoring and writing and over the years I have often encouraged her to unleash these gifts. I am extremely proud to see that she has finally done so in these Books "SEASONED FOR DESTINY" and I am confident that she will go on to author many more for the benefit of this generation and the generations to come.

Sally has a distinct Call to the Women in the Marketplace for whom has an undeniable burden, and her ability to reach out and offer herself to those women who suffer in silence, totally closed up, yet they really need someone they can trust and open up to.

Sally has addressed every type of Woman in these Books and the topics and subjects she has chosen to address are of great interest so she will reach and impact a very wide margin of Women, across the divide, locally and globally.

In other words, Sally has covered literally every subject that every Woman needs, to become well equipped and empowered for fulfilling Purpose and Destiny. More importantly she has done it in a manner that every Woman will identify with, because she has delved into the core basics of every issue without sugar coating the seriousness that one will require to commit to this journey to Destiny. Yet at the same time she has strongly encouraged every Woman by laying out the roadmap and by affirming and assuring her again and again, that she already has what it takes to master this journey and fulfil her Destiny.

Women from every sphere and sector will be awakened to the significance of their Callings and Destiny, giving them the incentive and motivation, they needed to forge on without giving up.

I have been in Christian ministry for over 45 years now and I have been humbled and privileged to minister to thousands of people Worldwide and to lead an organization with over 10, 000 partners locally and globally. The messages in these Books are central to the gospel that I myself preach because Destiny is God ordained.

I have no doubt that everyone who will read these Books will be greatly impacted and transformed, empowered and equipped to arise and lay hold of and fulfil that Destiny that each was born for.

Rev. Teresia Wairimu Kinyanjui.
Director& Founder,
Faith Evangelistic Ministry (FEM)

Endorsement

Destiny is one of the most misunderstood concepts today. Needless to say, the very mention of this word elicits feelings of inadequacy and anxiety among many. This has mainly been because of the complexity and mystery that seems to surround the understanding of what destiny is or is not.

In the 'Seasoned for Destiny' series, Sally wholeheartedly deliberates on the tenets that are to bring flavor and color to one's life. Reading through the pages it is clear that she empties her heart seeking to touch a heart at a time. This series specifically address the internal struggles that become stumbling blocks in the way of success for many and in particular women.

In today's world where everything is fast-paced and we all are confronted with many options; it is prudent that one finds their space and balance in life. Reading this book will motivate you to take a personal stock of where you are in the journey to destiny while recognizing and fixing the hindrances on the way.

To live a life of meaning and significance understanding Destiny is not an option but an expectation. As one who is passionate about women empowerment, I concur that clarity of purpose and calling, the fortitude to make available connections and the resilience to maintain success on the path of destiny can be overwhelming. This series is therefore an essential tool for one to make this valuable journey.

Her Excellency,

Rachel Ruto.

Spouse of the Deputy President,

Republic of Kenya.

Endorsement

I have known Sally from when she was about 5 years old and our relationship is firstly that of a mother and daughter. Beyond our family ties and now that Sally has grown to be a wife and mother with her own home, we have become very close friends and prayer partners and we are a great support and strength to one another in this journey to Destiny.

From an early age, Sally has demonstrated such a strong gift of expression and articulation. Sally is undeniably a gifted and anointed Servant of God who ministers the gospel passionately. She is also an inspirational coach and mentor to many women and girls from every walk of life. Her marketplace ministry has impacted many far and wide.

When Sally birthed her Seasoned Woman Forum about 7 years ago and as I witnessed her teachings, mentorship and coaching programs, I knew it would just be a matter of time before she consolidated those valuable teachings into books to reach a wider audience and sphere.

I think that every woman reading this book who will be transformed radically and propelled to fulfilling her Purpose and Destiny.

I am very passionate for Families and Nations, and a firm believer that strong healthy families are the foundation of strong healthy Nations. So, as I read these Books, I was deeply affected and encouraged by the manner in which Sally has tied up the value of the woman, not only as a leader, wealth creator, professional, career woman, but also as a family-oriented woman.

Any woman serious about fulfilling her Purpose and Destiny must be able to align her role as a family woman with her Purpose and Destiny and she must be cognizant of the fact that she cannot effectively impact Nations without first impacting families.

This series of books addresses every woman of every race, creed and color, and from any society and Nation, who desires to be and do all that she was born and created for.

Sally has adequately highlighted literally every dilemma and problem that a woman will encounter in the course of fulfilling her Purpose and Destiny, irrespective of her social status and standing in life, and she has given very practical solutions to these dilemmas and problems.

I would therefore urge every woman to read this Series of Books not only for her own equipping and empowerment but also for the equipping and empowerment of other women who she will share the contents of these book with.

Rev. Dr Judy Mbugua.
The Founder of the Homecare Spiritual Fellowship.

Endorsement

Sally Mahihu's book series "Seasoned for Destiny" is a clarion call for every woman, regardless of age, race or tribe, to discover her true identity, live out her deeper purpose and leave a legacy that younger generations are proud to remember. This book series is for such as time as this!"

(**Dr Herta von Stiegel, author of** *"The Mountain Within – Leadership Lessons and Inspiration for your Climb to the Top."*)

Endorsement

I am glad that Sally has followed through in writing this series of books titled **"Seasoned for Destiny"**. A couple of years ago, I gave her a word which I had received from the lord, that she would write some very significant books on issues pertaining to women in the marketplace.

These books will encourage and guide women greatly in understanding certain fundamentals that are related to their destiny such as business, career, leadership, relationships etc. Sally has captured literally every aspect of a modern woman's life, and she has taken time to address and analyze these issues in a way that every woman can identify with.

Sally has left no stone unturned in candidly addressing the subtle and not so subtle issues that often derail and delay many women from unleashing their full potential, to enable them to bring out their best selves.

I am persuaded that these books will change the lives of many women and will equip a new generation to become powerful agents of transformation in their spheres of influence.

Rev. Steve Pailthorpe

President of Crown Global, CEO of Iconic Digital & Senior Pastor of Crown Family Church

Introduction

I am fully persuaded that once a Woman understands who she was born to be and embraces the reason she was created (the Purpose for her being), then she will begin to live purposefully and intentionally towards it, and attain true fulfilment. And in so doing she will not only lay hold of her own Destiny, but she will also impact and propel many people, societies and Nations to their Purpose and Destiny as well.

This Series known as "<u>**SEASONED FOR DESTINY**</u>" consists of 5 Books namely:

Book 1 Your Naming And Defining,

Book 2 Your Calling And Positioning,

Book 3 Your Relationships And Networks,

Book 4 Your Making And Shaping and

Book 5 Your Harvests And Legacy.

- **BOOK 1** titled "**YOUR NAMING AND DEFINING**" deals with a Woman's identity, understanding "**the who**" she was born to be, it addresses her ability to embrace her true and authentic self. The chapters in this Book expound the various fundamentals regarding Identity and the power of Naming;

The Passwords to your true identity (understanding what should and what should not define you). The Triggers to an Identity Crisis, The Diary of a Destiny Diva, The Voices that shape and define you, The Destiny Queen or the Destiny Quitter, The Destiny Preserver or the Destiny Destroyer, The Destiny Clinger or the Destiny Kisser, The Destiny Connector or the Destiny Blocker, The Global Destiny Carrier or the Local Destiny Carrier, The Destiny Respecter or the Destiny Despiser, The Eagle Destiny or the Chicken Destiny, The Diary of a Destiny Diva and The Daily Confessions of a Destiny Chaser (on how to reinforce and affirm your identity daily with positive decrees and declarations).

- **BOOK 2** titled **"YOUR CALLING AND POSITIONING"** deals with a Woman's Calling and Purpose namely how to discover **"the what"** she was created to do, how to birth it and safeguard it, having a deep insight of what her purpose and calling entails, understanding how to access what she needs to fulfil it. This Book also it looks at the Woman's Positioning and Alignment on how to locate **"the where"** (in terms of sector or sphere) she is ordained to impact, how to navigate in that specific area and how to establish herself there. The chapters in this particular Book address the pertinent factors about Calling and Positioning namely; The Cues and Clues to her Calling, The Realities About her Calling, The Tools of a true Visionary, The steps to Birthing her Visions to Destiny, The Steps after Birthing her Visions to Destiny, The Pebble Stones in your High Heels to Destiny, The Arrows to her Place and sphere, The Snags and Snares in her Place and sphere, Establishing herself in the Place of Assignment and The Key Roles Of A Destiny Woman.

- **BOOK 3** titled **"YOUR RELATIONSHIPS AND NETWORKS"** deals with a Woman's relationships (networks and associations) namely "**the whom**" she should connect to, or disconnect from, for the sake of her Destiny. The chapters in this Book address; The Paradoxes In A Destiny Woman, Your Destiny Helpers, Your Destiny Killers, Your Sibling Rivals, Mastering The Art of Negotiation, The Spice Girls and Your Suspect Suitors.

- **BOOK 4** titled **"YOUR MAKING AND SHAPING"** deals with a Woman's moulding and sculpturing for Destiny namely "**the How**" of her preparation and equipping, and the various tests and trials she needs to undergo in order to fulfil her Purpose and Call as well as the principles, values and habits that inform her choices and decisions and refine her for Destiny. The chapters in this Book address and include; The Storms of a Destiny Survivor, The Scars of a Sculptured Woman, The Pain Patterns of a Destiny Champion, The Shape of a Destiny Diamond, The Trademarks of a Destiny Vessel, The Habits of a Destiny Addict, The Elegance of an Eagle Woman and The Pit-stops of a Destiny Racer.

- **BOOK 5** titled **"YOUR HARVESTS AND LEGACY"** deals with a Woman's legacy and the footprints she leaves behind for her generation and future generations. The chapters in this Book include; The Seasons of a Destiny Sower, Your Harvest In 7 Areas, Facts About Your Harvest, Hindrances To Your Harvest, Threats To Your Harvest, How To Respond To Your Harvest, Reasons Why You Get The Harvest, The Purpose Of Your Harvest, The Marks Of A Destiny Legend and A Woman's Defining Decades.

One of the main reasons for writing this Book was to consolidate the principles that I have been teaching, coaching and mentoring on over the years with regard to Purpose and Destiny.

Perhaps another compelling reason for writing this Series of Books is that every issue addressed here resonates within me personally, because these are issues I or people very close to me, continue to grapple with, and my sharing them here is for purposes of identifying my own personal struggles with those of the women I am addressing.

It is my sincere desire and hope that those who read this Series of Books will use the teachings to propel themselves to Destiny and to pass them on to other women, including those they are training, mentoring and coaching.

These Books will also form very valuable material for discussion groups whether as Book clubs, diverse groups within churches, corporate organisations and in all the various sectors and spheres of influence and hence the reason I have inserted "Destiny questions to ponder on" at the end of each chapter so that the interactive discussions can have a real impact on each reader and hopefully provoke them to apply the guidelines offered here in fulfilling their Purpose and Calling.

My sincere hope and expectation is that these Books are going to equip and empower every Woman desirous of fulfilling Purpose and to edify and assure her that no matter how hard the journey has been and no matter how much she has wanted to give up, she indeed has what it takes to finish this journey because she was designed for Destiny and she is already seasoned for it.

Although the target audience of this Series is primarily Women, it is now clear to me that even the men who come across them it will be equally impacted and equipped by the universal principles and the various topics addressed.

It is also my intention to target the young woman (older teens and young adults) because most of these principles and issues will greatly help these young women to avoid the mistakes that many of us older women made in our early years, and it will hopefully help the young woman to also avoid unnecessary delays in her journey to Destiny. It is therefore my sincere hope and prayer that every woman, young and old will read this Series of Books and be propelled to her Destiny.

The most fundamental aspect when embarking on your journey to Destiny is knowing "the **who you were born to be**" and coming to a place where you embrace your true and authentic self and walk securely in it because everything else thereafter regarding your Destiny hinges on this first revelation about your true self-identity.

These Books address, every Woman at whatever place she may be in her quest for Purpose and Destiny, the late Destiny bloomer, the Destiny dreamer and Destiny chaser, the Destiny wagon, the Destiny spectator, the Destiny backslider.

These Women are all desirous of living purposefully but they each struggle with different aspects about Destiny, whereby some may struggle with knowing and discovering '**the who**' and '**the what**' they were created to be (their self-identity and Calling), they go round in circles seeking '**the where**' they were assigned to influence (their place and sphere of assignment) and '**the whom**' they were designed to relate and connect with (the relationships), many of them get blindsided by the how they get made and formed (tests, trials and tribulations), while others navigate life steering dangerously without a road map seeking 'the which' (values and principles) they need to get there, while others become lethargic and burnout because they lack a sufficient conviction that the journey is worth the high price and sacrifice, they seem to be paying.

Every Woman's future after reading this Series of Books will be brightened by her assurance and confidence that she can now become the who she was born to be, do the what she was created to do, locate and position herself where she was sent to be an influence, relate and connect with the people that were assigned for her, surrender and embrace the process that will mould and make her into a vessel fit for Destiny, walk and align with the principles and values that she was intended to use to usher her to Destiny, lay hold of and effectively manage the successes, rewards and harvests that come with her faithfulness and diligence and leave footprints that will be a positive legacy for her generation and future generations.

What Is To Be Seasoned For Destiny?

For Purposes of this series of Books being "**Seasoned**" does not mean you have accomplished and "**arrived**" rather it means that you are passionate enough to lay hold of your Destiny, that you are ready to step forth by faith and embark on this epic journey just as you are; with the assurance that as you do so, the equipping and empowering you seek or need will be part and parcel of the journey.

… "**Being Seasoned for Destiny**" means that even though you occasionally struggle with who you are in the midst of a tumultuous dispensation that often seeks to swallow and drown you… **YET** you tenaciously fight to keep your head up, knowing that there is only one of you, and the only one you need to be, the one you were born to be.

… **"Being Seasoned for Destiny"** means that even though there are many raw and rough edges in your Character, that are still undergoing moulding and shaping… **YET** you continue to submit yourself to the skilful hands of the Master Potter, knowing that a **"Choice Vessel"** like you, will take longer to be formed because of the great impact and influence you will have on Nations and Generations.

… **"Being Seasoned for Destiny"** means that even though you have not quite mastered the Storms of life like failed relationships, chronic failures, loneliness, self-doubt and rejection, just to mention a few… **YET** you continue to brace yourself against those storms, choosing to dance in the rain; knowing that as you continue to set your sail in the wind of hope then ultimately, those storms will in fact become the very forces that will strengthen and propel you and bring you to that higher place of being alone, but not lonely, a place of self-knowledge, self-acceptance and self-assurance.

…. **"Being Seasoned for Destiny"** means that even though the seed of your womb has not germinated into the **"Daughters of Substance"** and **"Sons of Strength"** you had hoped for… **YET** you remain expectant that irrespective of any shortcomings in your parenting skills, or any unjust twist of fate, your resilience as a praying mother is never in vain and in due season, your Sons and Daughters will manifest into a Seasoned Generation, that will shake cities and impact Nations.

… **"Being seasoned for Destiny"** means that even though you may constantly be in a financial mess and distress, until you feel so desperate and drained… **YET** you refuse to despair knowing that your hands are anointed to create wealth and as you continue to trust, embrace and practice sound godly wealth creating habits and principles, then surely the floodgates of heaven will fling open and usher you into unprecedented financial freedom.

… "**Being Seasoned for Destiny** "means that even though the dire consequences of your **poor choices**, have come to haunt you and you are paying the painful price of your past folly under a heavy cloak of remorse… YET you keep your head lifted up high knowing that as you appreciate the lessons learned from your past folly, then this too will pass; because your harsh and ugly Winter must ultimately surrender to your soft and beautiful Spring that will come with forbearance and Second Chances.

… "**Being Seasoned for Destiny**" means that perhaps your inner joy is being dampened by the anguish and agony of a sick body…. YET you forge on, smiling through your pain knowing that as long as you have a Purpose and Assignment, that you are committed to fulfil and a Destiny to lay hold of, then your Creator will preserve you and keep you, until you are done.

…"**Being Seasoned for Destiny**" means that even though your walk with God is like a seesaw, characterised by some seasons of intense (almost fanatical) passion and commitment and a radical faith, but also with other seasons of panic, doubt, or even silent indignation when things do not go the way you thought… YET you pick yourself up every time and dust off the doubt and purge your panic, and with hot blinding tears, you make a decision to hope and trust anyway, knowing that He who began a good work in you is able to complete it.

…"**Being Seasoned For Destiny**" means that even though you have encountered Chronic failures and disappointment… YET it is about finding the grace to deal with the many disappointments of life and finding the resolve to regain missed seasons and lost opportunities, it is about finding the strength to reposition yourself for a new beginning, because a Seasoned Woman knows, that while there is life, there is hope and while there is hope, there is always another chance to rise again and forge on to fulfil her Destiny.

... **"Being Seasoned for Destiny"** means that even though you come to the end of yourself **YET** your find a song in your heart that keeps you going when the journey gets tough and this is the song that will keep her going even when the storms rage and the fiery furnace flares.

The Seasoned Woman knows…

Who she really is…

The Purpose for which she was created…

She is uniquely gifted…

She does not allow her failures…

And successes to define her…

She confidently says…

When I grow up I want to be Me!

The Seasoned Woman knows…

She is fearfully and wonderfully made…

With a true beauty inside her…

Reflected in her whole life lived…

The Seasoned Woman clothes herself…

In dignity, honesty, integrity, patience, kindness, mercy and love…

The Seasoned Woman has learnt…

To embrace the seasons of her life…

Allow them to mould and sculpt her...

Into a vessel of strength, honour and dignity...

She is a Woman of all Seasons...

A vessel of strength, honour and dignity...

She has learnt to weather and survive the storms of her daily life...

Having the grace to dance in the rain...

To smile through her pain...

She has risen to define life...

The strength to rise like a phoenix from the ashes...

The Seasoned Woman has passion for her Nation...

She has solutions for her Generation...

And she has the welfare of her people at heart...

She is a voice to the voiceless...

So, as you reflect and take stock of all the myriad of Seasons you may have encountered so far in your journey to Destiny, remember that you are **"So Totally Seasoned"** for your Destiny and that nothing shall by any means prevent you, from finishing your Race and not only finishing it, but finishing strong... so soldier on **Woman of Destiny**, until you reach the finish line.

Chapter 1

PROCESSED FOR DESTINY

Trusting The Process of Your Moulding and Making

Chapter Preview

1. *Knowing And Owning Your True Identity and Name is a Process*

2. *Discovering And Fulfilling Your Purpose And Calling Is A Process*

3. *Locating Your Right Positioning is a Process*

4. *Identifying Your Right Relationships And Connections is a Process*

5. *Setting And Establishing Your Values And Principles is a Process*

6. *Your Preparation And Equipping Is A Process*

7. *Your Rewarding is a Process*

OPENING REMARKS

"The process is the most important part of the journey. Appreciate it while you have it." ~ Unknown

Becoming equipped to fulfil your Purpose and Destiny is a process and a journey which you must embrace and allow, because having a Call and Purpose is one thing, but your character, gifting and skills will need to be harnessed over time through certain processes.

Provided you are committed and open and desire to become more and more effective in fulfilling your Calling then your process of making will propel you to levels of effectiveness you never dreamt of.

"Hold the Vision, trust the process." Unknown

The process is of course painful and sometimes you may feel you cannot take anymore and you may get tempted to quit and step out and quit but you must keep in mind that the process is necessary and without it your Calling will at best be mediocre, and not fully fulfilled.

There are various **pain points** in your life that cause a sharp pain in one area of your life or another and these pain points must be addressed and dealt with as part of your process so as to free you to move swiftly to your Destiny.

You will also undergo various **seasons** that will mould your character and equip you for Destiny, such as seasons of barrenness and waiting, training and preparation, purging and pruning, celebrating the success of others while your own is still illusive, seasons of transition and change, sowing and investing without seeing any returns, and finally your season of victory and breakthrough etc.

There are **painful wounds** from your past that may not have healed and which you need to address and seek healing from and where they have healed then those wounds have turned into **scars,** which scars you need to spin into stars in order to fulfil your Calling and Destiny.

There are **vicious storms** that you will encounter such as storms of parenthood, financial storms, relational storms, storms of loss, storms of sickness etc. that you must master, and come out stronger and wiser in order to fulfil your Calling and Destiny.

There are some **surgeries** that you will need to undergo from the top of your head to the souls of your feet which will radically refine you and enable you to align your whole self to your Purpose and Destiny.

There are some **gravel stones** in your high heels symbolizing some hindrances within you that you will need to deal with so that they do not slow your journey to Destiny.

Your ability to respond appropriately to these challenges during your process and forming will empower you to fulfil your Purpose and Destiny more effectively. It is important that you embrace the process and forming no matter how painful it may be. After coming out of the fiery furnace you will be as good as gold and after you allow every dross to be scraped out of you, you will be as pure as silver.

"We should focus on our process, not on the outcome of our processes." ~ Unknown

Your alabaster jar is a prized possession and your Destiny will require all the contents in your alabaster jar.

You will have grace for the process, grace covers your eyes from what you are going through so that you can handle the weight that you would normally not be able to handle.

Phil. 1:6 – *"…being confident of this very thing, that He who has begun a good work in you will complete it until the day of Jesus Christ…"*

1. KNOWING AND OWNING YOUR TRUE IDENTITY AND NAME IS A PROCESS

The quest for your true identity and your true name will not come overnight because it is a journey of self-discovery that will take you time even as your self-awareness becomes stronger and you become more articulate in understanding the who you were born to be.

2. DISCOVERING AND FULFILLING YOUR PURPOSE AND CALLING IS A PROCESS

Firstly, your calling and Purpose will not be revealed to you in one go, but through a series of puzzles that you will gradually put together one by one until you begin to have a more comprehensive picture of what your Calling and Purpose is. Secondly fulfilling it will require steps and procedures that will entail a journey.

3. LOCATING YOUR RIGHT POSITIONING IS A PROCESS

Positioning yourself in your right place and sphere is not a one-time action but a continuous deliberate and intentional process that takes time as you navigate that place understanding its nature, understanding the people already positioned there, understanding the cultures and protocols etc.

4. IDENTIFYING YOUR RIGHT RELATIONSHIPS AND CONNECTIONS IS A PROCESS

Perhaps one of the most delicate processes you will have to undergo in your journey to Destiny is identifying and discerning the specific relationships that are your portion and that are intended to influence and shape you for Destiny. Understanding how to develop such relationships, relate to them appropriately and maintain them is also a process. In addition, discerning those relationships that are counterproductive and that will derail you from your journey to Destiny so that you may disconnect wisely but radically is an even more critical process.

5. SETTING AND ESTABLISHING YOUR VALUES AND PRINCIPLES IS A PROCESS

Fulfilling your Calling and entering your Desitny must be accomplished in a proper manner and you must walk and carry yourself in a way that befits an honorouble vessel of honour. You will therefore need to set and establish values, codes, ethics etc. upon which you will base your choices and decisions and this in itself is a process.

6. YOUR PREPARATION AND EQUIPPING IS A PROCESS

At the beginning of your journey to Desiny you will basically have what it takes like gifts, talents, skills etc. but in their raw form and you will therefore need them to be harnessed and sharpened so as to make you effective. You may have the passion for your Destiny but passion without character will not get you far so there will be a process of moulding and sculpturing your character etc.

7.   YOUR REWARDING IS A PROCESS

In the course of fulfilling your Purpose and Calling faithfully you will receive rewards in the form of promotions, greater influence and impact, wealth and prosperity, growth in every area of your life etc. and this will not happen overnight but through a process that will ultimately usher you to Destiny.

Destiny Questions to Ponder on

1. *Do you believe that the process of knowing who you are is complete?*

2. *What part of the process of discovering and fulfilling your Purpose and Calling have you found most challenging?*

3. *What hindrances and obstacles may have delayed the process of your positioning?*

4. *Which process was more challenging: connecting from your right relationships or disconnecting from your wrong relationships?*

5. *How have your values and principles helped you in your decision-making process?*

6. *What part of your preparation and equipping process did you have to repeat and why?*

7. *What has been your response to your rewarding process?*

Chapter 2

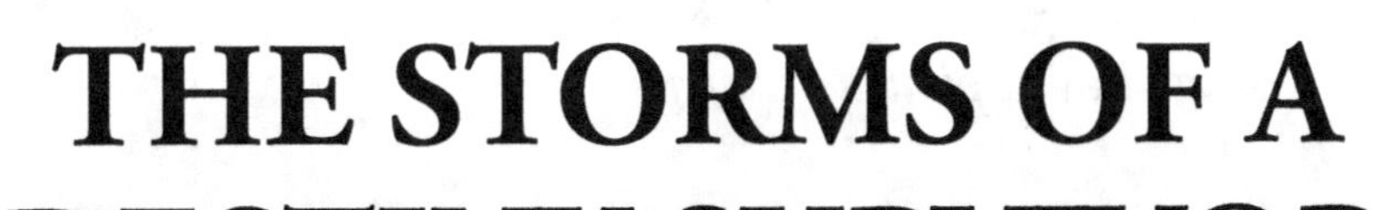

THE STORMS OF A DESTINY SURVIVOR

Weathering the Storms of Life and Coming Through Stronger

Chapter Preview

OPENING REMARKS

"You will not be the same after the storms of life; you will be stronger, wiser and more alive than ever before." Bryant McGill

Storms are often a symbol of adversity or hardship that we face in our lives from time to time that threaten to take us out.

As you seek to fulfil your Purpose and walk to your Destiny you will inevitably encounter various storms which will hurl and bash you against the rocks mercilessly. Your ability to acknowledge that there will be storms in your journey, will give you the right mind-set and attitude to confront, face and survive those storms. Despite the bruises you will walk away with, suffice you do not allow any storm in your life to jeopardize, delay or abort your Purpose and Destiny.

The different types of storms you will encounter in your life will range from storms in your **relationships**, storms in your **finances**, storms in your **health**, storms from the **death** of loved ones, **reputational** storms, and **spiritual** storms arising from your walk with God.

Remember that there is a Purpose for every storm you encounter in your life sometimes it is because you've taken the wrong path in your journey, due to wrong choices and decisions and you have disregarded specific principles and guidelines as to how you should fulfil your Purpose and Destiny and you need redirecting back to the right path.

Failure to learn the lessons in this kind of storm, means it will continue until we learn what we are supposed to.

And perhaps most comforting of all about some storms, is they come to empower, equip and to impact you, in certain areas that you need strengthening in your life such as faith and trust, so that when things get tough and rough in your life, you must learn to stand strong despite your circumstances.

Sometimes the storm is necessary to save you from worse dangers that threaten your Destiny like where, after great accomplishments and successes, you begin to show signs of being self-sufficient or prideful, confidence in self and the seedlings of an arrival mentality whereby you retreat into a comfort zone.

So, a storm comes to wake you up and to keep you alert and sober, and to remind you that the journey is not over and there is still a lot to be done in fulfilling your Purpose and Destiny.

As Bishop T.D Jakes often observes, storms can leave you disoriented and disappointed, quietly bitter and wounded and in benign resignations and you begin to wonder what happened to the hopes and dreams that used to burn within you. Sometimes you may hide behind a smile and a vivacious personality but with an inner ache and a piercing cry for help, because a relentless storm is raging within you.

"Don't be discouraged by the storm. When it's all said and done, you may go through it, but you will come out standing strong."
~Joel Osteen

The key is to understand how to master the storms in your life and to not only survive those storms but to thrive during the storms and to use those storms to your advantage whereby you come out of them stronger, wiser, more equipped and prepared to handle future storms. Most importantly to let that storm propel you and usher you to a higher level where you are more effective transformational and impactful as you fulfil your Purpose and Destiny so that at the end of the day the storms do not master you but you master them.

Mastering the storm will however require you to learn how to discern and smell when a storm is brewing in whichever area of your life and like in any physical storm to prepare for it. You should seek shelter in the right people such as your Destiny helpers, the right places mentally and emotionally so that you adopt the right mind set and calm emotions and the right things such as your values and principles that will shield and protect you from total destruction in the storm.

This way even though you may get bruises the storm will not destroy you, this means positioning yourself in the 'eye' of the storm where there is safety and where the viciousness of whatever storm you are facing such as financial distress, dysfunctions or rebellion in your children, marital havoc etc. can propel you out and upwards into a higher level of thinking and responding to those situations and thereby overpowering the storm.

Perhaps one important final thing when facing the storms is to learn how to **"clean the mess"** after the storm, because just like a physical storm, any storm in your life will leave **'debris'** like wounded emotions and unmet expectations, painful disappointments and confusion which you must address and overcome for you to continue fulfilling your Purpose and Destiny.

The sooner you clean up the physical debris that is left by a physical storm the better, so too, the sooner you clean up the **"emotional debris"** left by your personal storms, the better.

You must Purpose to heal and move on because like the physical debris, emotional debris if not cleaned and removed remains as messy obstacles that will constantly trip you and block your way forward towards fulfilling your Purpose and Destiny.

Suffice to say that storms come to mould and shape us so no matter how painful they may be and how destructive they appear, ultimately the intention is not to destroy us.

1. CALMING RELATIONSHIP STORMS

"No relationship is all sunshine, but two people can share one umbrella and survive the storm together." ~Unknown

All your relationships whether family, professional, business, social, or romantic will undergo storms at one point or another and this can be emotionally devastating. It can take its toll on you seriously destabilizing you and your ability to remain balanced and on course in fulfilling your Purpose and entering your Destiny.

Storms in your professional relationships can arise out of unmet expectations and breach of ethics etc. and impact negatively on your career, while storms in your business relationships can arise out of poor planning dishonest dealings etc. and can rock and capsize your finances. Storms in your social relationships, can arise out of betrayal and breach of trust etc. and can seriously affect your self-esteem and confidence especially where there is rejection and abandonment, and storms in your spiritual relationships may seriously affect your walk and relationship with God, your faith as well as your relationship with other brethren.

So, the key is to acknowledge and confront the issues affecting your relationships towards seeking solutions and healing and restoration, instead of keeping them locked up within you.

Perhaps the best advice for managing relational storms irrespective of whichever nature of relationship, is to be deliberate and intentional in our choice of friendships, whether they be female friendships, professional colleagues, business partners, social welfare groups etc. So, you establish clear values and principles as well as a criteria as to how you will carefully select the people in these relationships.

Ensure to determine your value relevance and expectations and those of the other party in each relationship, so that you have clarity and less room for conflict and confusion as you go along.

It may be more difficult when it comes to family and some crucial Destiny relationships that you may not have the luxury to really choose and select, neither will you have the luxury to just walk out of them at will, but at least you can master the art of managing them effectively and fruitfully.

However, when these relationship storms do come in whatever area, then the best way to calm them is to identify the triggers and causes; address the issues calmly choosing the right timing, seek help from trusted experts or friends. Aim to seek solutions and be realistic if the relationship must end, or be put on hold for a while.

A sizeable percentage of marriages will undergo storms, maybe due to infidelity, spousal abuse etc. Some may survive, some may not, and yours may not be an exception.

As a Woman of Destiny who has allowed the storms of life to sculpt and mould you then your strategy is to survive a marital storm without becoming embittered, cynical and a hater of love and life. Over time, other storms of life have built a strong character within you of a storm survivor who knows that there will be pain and loss along the way which does not need to destroy and kill you.

You must always Purpose to be stronger than your pain and powerful enough to master your every storm.

"The couples that are meant to be, are the ones who go through everything that is meant to tear them apart, and come out even stronger." Unknown

So, ensure you do not allow any of these storms to jeopardize, delay or abort your Purpose and Destiny.

2. NAVIGATING THE STORMS OF PARENTHOOD

"The hardest part of being a parent is that you can't stop the world from hurting your child. You can only be there to ease the pain." ~Unknown

Perhaps this is one of the most painful of all storms for those with children because everyone goes out of her way to do her level best to raise sons of strength and daughters of dignity.

She sacrifices and pays a high price willingly in the course of her parenting because she wants the very best for her children and while she will admit that she made some mistakes along the way, she nonetheless does not expect the fruit of her womb (that she loves with all that is within her) could possibly turn out to be such a pain and sorrow.

The pain of a child being destroyed by drugs or other vices of life is all too much for a mother to bear, because it is in the heart of every mother to desire the best for her child and she makes very serious sacrifices for her child. When the unexpected storm hits her and her child it may throw her out of balance reeling with pain because she cannot imagine that the little child she cradled and curdled could have turned into someone she does not even recognize.

Other times the pain comes from seeing your child get hurt or slowly destroyed by a wrong relationship and there is nothing you can do because your advice is falling on deaf ears or where the ugly claws of sickness, disease or deformity attack your child and you watch helplessly as their hopes and dreams are shattered. Those storms are almost unbearable.

Nonetheless as a Woman of Destiny who knows her and her child must be preserved for the sake of fulfilling their Destiny then she holds on stubbornly with a radical faith and hopes that no matter what her children may go through ultimately the tide will turn and she will live to rejoice at the redemption of her children as they get restored and fulfil their Destiny.

Every Woman who has gone through these painful parenthood storms will no doubt have been advised by older and more experienced parents, that sometimes-tough love (no matter how much it may pain you) may be the best solution especially where you may have to let go of your young adult child (where spanking and punishing is no longer the answer).

Allow them to take the "prodigal route" and if necessary, swim in the miry clay with the 'pigs' until they come to a revelation of their destructive ways and make a turnaround either because logic and common sense has hit them or because you chose to remain on your knees for that child (confessing the word of God that since you have done your best to raise that child in the right ways and though they may depart from them nonetheless they will always revert and not get destroyed).

Proverbs 22:6 – *"Train up a child in the way he should go, and when he is old, he will not depart from it."*

Seeking wise counsel from your Destiny helpers who have endured parenthood storms and survived, will greatly help you and encourage you to also endure and wait out such storms.

Sometimes as difficult as it is to accept, the best way to survive these storms of parenthood is to totally surrender your child to God because it is God who gave you that child in the first place. God's love and concern for your child is far greater than yours and God's plan for your child and His desire in ensuring that those plans are fulfilled are far greater than your own desire for that child.

Always keep in mind that God's power to reach your child even in the darkest place and His power to lead that child out of whatever abyss and pit is far greater than the devil's power to keep holding or misleading your child.

3. MANAGING FINANCIAL STORMS

"We have to make tough choices. We have moved forward despite some financial hardships." ~ *Chris McCloud*

When you have people depending on you financially the loss and lack of finances and material resources can destabilize you and spiral you out of control as those who depend on you look at you helplessly.

"Do not leave yourself and your family unprotected against financial storms... build up savings." ~ ***Ezra Taft Benson***

Sometimes the financial storm may come as a result of your own negligence, bad stewardship. Sometimes it may just be pure misfortune, being conned and swindled and betrayed in circumstances that were beyond your control.

Sometimes you may enter into relationships, whether social, romantic, professional or business where the other party may deceive and steal from you or that person may cause you to incur financial debts and liabilities through reckless or ignorant application or the investment of your funds. You find yourself in financial distress whereby the chances of recovery from that person or those persons is virtually impossible.

At other times you may have been a financial dependent on someone say a spouse or a parent or your child who suddenly is not there and you have no idea how to pick up the pieces and move on.

A financial storm is where you undergo shame and embarrassment because of the public exposure, you may also undergo bankruptcy where you lose your credibility and other areas of your life are affected like you cannot hold a public position of leadership in many countries when you are bankrupt, also the lack of resources paralyses you from even continuing to fulfil your Purpose and Destiny.

Irrespective of why you ended up in a financial storm i.e., whether it was self-inflicted or externally inflicted, the important thing is to survive that storm and to ensure that it does not destroy you by remembering that you are not defined by money or material substance nor by how wealthy you are or how poor you are because you are so much more than that.

The other thing to remember is that money comes and money goes and that if you had succeeded in building up finances or creating wealth before, then you can do it again suffice to say you will just make different and better choices.

Some of the lessons you will learn out of financial storms is that if it was because of being conned or swindled then you will be careful to select who you deal with next time and you will be careful to do proper research and due diligence.

If it was due to your bad stewardship or mismanagement then you will learn to be a better money manager next time and if it was due to vain indulgences, you will learn self-control and discipline in how and on what you spend your money.

Ultimately the key is not to allow money to master you but instead you learn to master money so that it works for you instead of you working for it. Seek advice and wise counsel from the many experts on money matters.

4.   HEALING FROM THE STORMS OF SICKNESS

"Your illness does not define you. Your strength and courage does." ~ Unknown

Sometimes it is your own health or the health of a loved one that may creep in slowly or suddenly to totally disorient you and destabilize you and paralyze you until you are unable to continue effectively in your journey to Destiny.

For some women their own sickness and affliction may not be as devastating as that of a loved one such as a spouse and a child or a parent. Terminal sicknesses that go on for a very long time can take a serious toll on you and your family emotionally, mentally and financially. It can cause such stress that will strain relationships to breaking point because of differences in how the situation should be approached etc. especially where hearts are already hurting.

The worst aspect of it is maybe where there is a clear indication that the sick person whether it is you or a loved one will eventually die but there is resistance and denial which adds to the pain.

You must Purpose that the storms of sickness will not derail you from the course of your journey to Destiny and you must not allow the embers of hope to die within you.

One of the possible solutions of surviving storms of sickness (whether it is your own sickness or that of a loved one), is ensuring that you and your loved ones are in the same place regarding God's miraculous ability to heal while at the same time not being in denial about the existence of the sicknesses and the practical action that might be needed.

In addition, discussing and agreeing on the methods and modes of treatment that are appropriate under the circumstances, as well as the sharing of responsibilities and burdens during this difficult time.

It is also important to ensure that you adopt measures of self-care to ensure that you remain strong and healthy when taking care of a sick loved one.

"Sometimes life doesn't turn out the way you may have wanted it and chronic illness can alter even the best laid plans, but that shouldn't hold you back from your future." ~**Peter Waite**

Perhaps one of the strongest motivations and encouragements when undergoing the storms of sickness is by constantly reminding yourself that your Purpose and Destiny will preserve you and your loved ones and that you will survive this storm of sickness because you still have a Purpose and Destiny to fulfil.

5. RECOVERING FROM STORMS OF LOSS AND SORROW

"I think the hardest part of losing someone is not having to say goodbye, but rather learning to live without them. Always trying to fill the void, the emptiness that's left inside your heart when they go." ~ Ameer Hasan

At other times, it will be a devastating tragedy either a sudden accident or worse still a suicide of a loved one that leaves you reeling with disbelief but you must find the strength and fortitude to pick up the pieces and gather yourself and move on.

The storms of loss and sorrow through the death of a loved one are perhaps the most devastating because no matter what you do that person cannot come back to you and it is you to recover from the sorrow and pain of that loss.

The pain, anguish and trauma may persist and become compounded over a long period of time which then affects your ability to fulfil your Purpose and Destiny so that beyond the tragedy of losing a loved one you also abort your Purpose and delay your Destiny.

It is therefore important to make a deliberate decision and choice that this storm of life will not cause a double tragedy and that recovering from it and forging on to fulfil your Purpose and Destiny is perhaps one way of healing by defocusing from the pain and sorrow and to avoid falling into a depression.

In fact, the excitement and joy of fulfilling your Purpose will be in itself a pain reliever to some extent when you imagine how happy your departed loved one would be if they knew you were continuing to be **"the who"** you were born to be and **"the what"** you were created to do.

Seeking help from experts and adopting proven, coping mechanisms is of course necessary.

6. RESTORATION FROM REPUTATIONAL STORMS

Your reputation is the beliefs and opinions that people generally hold about you, including the widespread belief that you possess certain characteristics. It includes your name, your image, your label, your standing in society and how others see you, based on the image you have built and reflected overtime.

"You can't buy a good reputation; you must earn it." ~Harvey MacKay

So, your reputation can either be a good one or a bad one.

"It takes 20 years to build a reputation and five minutes to ruin it. If you think about that, you'll do things differently." ~ Warren Buffet

A time may come when you may undergo a public scandal either arising out of your own wrongdoing or from false accusations or victimization with regard to either allegations of moral impropriety, bribery, corruption or whatsoever, which tarnishes your name and throws you into an ugly limelight of shame, guilt, regret and ridicule. This affects not only you but your loved ones, your career, profession, business etc. and this can culminate in a nasty reputational storm over a period of time.

For many women, a good reputation and character are important because it is what clothes you with the desired honour, respect and credibility. In fact, most women will sacrifice a lot in order to safeguard and maintain a good reputation, but sometimes if that good spick and span reputation begins to get in the way of your Purpose and Destiny either because it becomes a point of pride, self-righteousness, a critical and harsh judgmental spirit on others whereby you become intolerant to the weaknesses of others and you are unable to accord or extend any grace or empathy. Then you may need to go through a shakeup… otherwise known as a reputational storm.

Or where you begin to credit yourself and give that good reputation an exaggerated place in your life and you begin to base your entire identity on your ability to maintain a good reputation then it means that when that good reputation is tarnished and smeared under whatever circumstances then your identity suffers and you fall into an identity crisis.

A reputational storm may therefore come to shake that over dependence on people's views and opinions of you and to instead teach you to base your confidence on the who you know you were born to be (which is your true identity) and on the what you were created to do (meaning your Calling and Destiny).

This storm will also teach you that you are not defined by other people's views and opinions whether they be positive or negative.

Suffice to say that a good reputation is an asset that you should indeed build and maintain but in the unfortunate event that your good reputation suffers a storm, then having a revelation that your value and relevance is based on much more than your good reputation will help you survive that storm.

Having a clear focus and passion for your Calling and Destiny and a strong determination to fulfil it will greatly help you in recovering from any reputational storms. In addition, when you already have a strong inner good character then that character cannot be shaken and it is more entrenched than your reputation.

"Worry about your character not your reputation. Your character is who you are, your reputation is who people think you are."
John Wooden

You will be able to survive a reputational storm because of the ability to forgive yourself for why your reputation got tarnished and your ability to take responsibility for your behaviour and actions (where the loss of your good reputation was self-inflicted) and moving on with a decision to do differently next time, guarding what relationships you associate with etc.

Your ability to develop certain life skills and coping mechanisms and the ability to walk in a healthy self-awareness, will determine how quickly you come out of this storm and how much damage you will be able to control, as you seek to have your good reputation restored.

Ensure you do not allow any of these storms to jeopardize, delay or abort your Purpose and Destiny.

7.   RISING ABOVE SPIRITUAL STORMS

"The storms and winds that were meant to hold you back and break you. God will use them to thrust you forward." ~ Unknown

This is where you encounter a shake-up in your spiritual walk with God, either because your faith is shaken following some events that may leave you frustrated, and disappointed. You begin to question the existence of God, his love and faithfulness, or where due to your own disobedience and rebellion you find yourself in undesirable and uncomfortable waters out of the path of your Purpose and Destiny, and out of the will of God.

A spiritual storm may also come in the form of broken divine connections with your spiritual leaders and authorities or other brethren due to whatever reasons. Owning and taking responsibility for your own sins and wrongs. Forgiving and seeking forgiveness will enable you to survive such storms and even learn some valuable lessons that will empower you to fulfil your Purpose and Destiny.

"Some people create their own storms and then get upset when it rains." ~ Unknown

In addition, spiritual storms may come when you have subjected yourself knowingly or unknowingly to wrong teachings and doctrines or even cults or where your walk with God has become based on religion, do's and don'ts and legalistic rules instead of being based on an intimate relationship with God. At that point God may need to allow a shake up so that everything erroneous, defiled and contaminated may be removed out of you so that you can return and embrace that which is pure, true and emanates from God Himself. This may involve a threshing or a purging.

During such storms and to avoid the enemy taking advantage, you must remain connected to people who are your Destiny helpers and who love you and who can walk with you through this stormy time as opposed to isolating yourself or surrounding yourself with the wrong people.

You must be careful not to start hosting pity parties or fall into a victim syndrome when God is threshing and purging you because he is doing it for your good and to enable you be aligned for fulfilling your Purpose and Destiny.

"God sends the storm to show that He is the only shelter." ~ Unknown

Destiny Questions to Ponder On

1. *Which storms have you encountered so far in your journey to Destiny?*

2. *In order of priority which of these storms do you consider most challenging?*

3. *Are you currently going through any storm, if so which one and how are you coping?*

4. *Which of the storms in your life do you believe were self-generated/inflicted?*

5. *Are there storms that you believe one can prevent, if so which ones and how?*

6. *What kind of measures would you advice someone to take when dealing with a financial storm?*

7. *Did any of the storms empower you once you were out of them, if so, how?*

This Page Was Intentionally Left Blank

Chapter 3

THE SCARS OF A SCULPTURED WOMAN

Turning Your Scars Into Stars

Chapter Preview

1. *From the Cold Alleys of Abandonment to the Highway of Acceptance.*
2. *From the Deep Lake of Loss to the Landscape of life*
3. *From the Shackles of Shame to the Halls of Honour*
4. *From the Abyss of Abuse to the Armchair of Affirmation*
5. *From the Gallows of Gross-Injustice to the Gates of Equity*
6. *From the Pits of Poverty to the Mines of Abundance*
7. *From the Backyard of Betrayal to the Lounge of Loyalty*

OPENING REMARKS

In the physical and natural a wound is an injury that causes a tear, a deep cut and pain. Once wounds are healed, they leave marks known as scars.

Beyond the physical visible scars, we get from physical injury and surgery are other scars that are not visible but probably more painful and deeper because they affect us mentally and emotionally etc. These invisible scars arise from painful and traumatic incidents and events that happened in our lives under various circumstances due to various factors that wounded us emotionally or mentally and overtime those wounds may begin to heal but the scars remain (reminding us of that wounded past).

In life we will get many wounds as we journey to Destiny, however don't ever be ashamed of the scars that those wounds left you with. A scar means the hurt is over and the wound is healed and closed. It means you conquered the pain, learned a lesson, grew stronger, and moved forward. A scar is the tattoo of a triumph to be proud of.

Don't allow your wounds and the resulting scars to hold you hostage and don't allow them to make you live your life in fear because you can't make the scars in your life disappear, but you can change the way you see them and you can start seeing your scars as a sign of strength and not pain.

"Out of suffering, have emerged the strongest souls; the most massive characters are seared with scars." ~ Kahlil Gibran

So, see your scars as a sign of how you survived and you have your scars to prove it and you now have a chance to grow even stronger.

Scars have the strange power to remind us that our past is real and they show us where we have been but they do not dictate where we are going.

Learn to brand your scars into stars that shine bright and show others how to survive and thrive despite the scars.

In order to heal from the wounds (and brand the scars that they left, into stars) we must first, acknowledge that we have those scars, ascertain what caused our scars, then we confront them, towards healing and branding them into stars.

"My scars tell a story. They are a reminder of times when life tried to break me, but failed. They are markings where the structure of my character was welded." ~ **Steve Maraboli**

There are at least **seven steps** one would take in treating a physical wound in the natural, which are the same steps one would take symbolically to treat emotional and mental wounds;

- A physical wound must be **cleaned** constantly and **disinfected** to avoid it getting dirty, which will lead to it being septic and infected and thereby delay healing. Likewise, when you are emotionally wounded, you must ensure to constantly **purify** your emotions and mind-set by rejecting and casting out any toxicity and negativity, selfish agendas and motives because that will make your wounds to remain raw and hinder healing.

- With a physical wound you must **stop the bleeding** by **bandaging** and **dressing** the wound because blood is a vital life sustaining substance needed in your body and you cannot afford to keep losing. Likewise, when you are emotionally wounded, you must **seek to address the hurt and pain** by embracing and covering with whatever will stop it namely having the right thoughts, the right confessions over yourself and surrounding yourself with the right relationships.

- Where a physical wound is deep, it will need **stitching** to close up the skin and avoid the tear and cut from getting wider. The stitching is painful and you may need something to numb the area around the wound so as to avoid you suffering the pain of the stitching. Likewise with emotional wounds that go very deep (e.g., Sexual or severe physical abuse) the painful stitching symbolizes the need for expert and professional treatment like seasons of **deep therapy** that may be very painful because it requires you to address those traumatic events. Sometimes your response to your traumatic events that happened to you can cause more damage to you than the actual painful event itself. So, the "stitching" symbolizes closing up the wounds completely to avoid them reopening.

- With a physical wound **antibiotic** will be used to accelerate its healing and avoid any inner infection. Likewise, you must counter the ugly effects of emotional wounds by using **antidotes** like faith instead of fear, trust instead of doubt, love instead of hate, forgiveness instead of grudge etc.

- A physical wound is kept **covered** once it has been cleaned and disinfected so as to avoid further external injury when you come into contact with physical items that may cut or tear the wound again which will make it worse. Likewise, when you are emotionally wounded and you are doing your best to purify your emotions and mind set, you should **"cover"** your wounds with the right influences (people who will empathize with you and encourage you) and avoid the wrong influences (people who will mock and taunt you).

- With a physical wound you will usually get a **tetanus shot/injection** to reinforce and further protect you from getting bacterial infection (especially where the wound may have been caused by rusty sharp objects or burns or even animal bites), and that tetanus shot may be painful. Likewise, when you are emotionally wounded you may need to be **rebuked** and **counseled** with some sharp painful truths (especially where your wounding was as a result of your wrong choices and actions) and such rebukes will prevent you from making those wrong choices and actions in the future.

- As a physical wound continues to heal, it has to be constantly **watched to check** and treat any recurring or hidden infections until the wound is completely healed. Likewise with emotional wounds, you must constantly **keep watch** over your emotions and mind-sets to avoid returning to toxicity and negativity. This means that with both a physical and an emotional wound you must not stop the treatment and the healing process prematurely and you must allow the wounds to heal completely.

For a physical wound, once the wound has healed and the pain is over only a physical mark remains, a scar which will teach you some lessons namely to avoid whatever it is that caused that physical injury whether it was internally or externally inflicted. Likewise for emotional wounds the scars remain as a reminder that you survived and you lived to learn valuable lessons.

So, wherever your pains and wounds may have come from, whether it be from the cold alleys of abandonment, the backyard of betrayal, pits of poverty, abyss of abuse, lakes of loss, shackles of shame or gallows of gross-injustice, the most effective way to heal so that you can brand the scars from that pain and those wounds into stars is to:

Firstly, hate the thing that caused the pain and wounds with a perfect hatred to enable you become an advocate that will fight against it in the lives of other people. You must never become or behave like those people who wounded you, meaning that if you ever find yourself wounding other people in the same way that you were wounded then you must stop immediately and break that cycle.

Secondly, purpose to turn each one of those ugly wounds into the exact opposite so that you will not be known, as the Woman who was abandoned as a child but as a Woman who accepts and cherishes those who have been abandoned or are prone to abandonment.

Instead of being known as a victim of abuse be known as a victor of care and concern for those who are victims of abuse or are prone to abuse.

Instead of being known as one who suffered loss or become known as one who lost, be known as one who gains by loving.

Instead of being known as one who was betrayed, purpose to be known as one who is loyal and one who encourages others to be loyal.

Instead of being known as one who was crippled by poverty, purpose to be known as one who is prosperous and empowers others to climb out of the pit of poverty.

Instead of being known as one who was a prisoner of gross-injustice, purpose to be known as one who is just and fair.

Instead of being known as one who was bound by shackles, shame, purpose to become known as one who is free and one who walks with honour.

Thirdly, remember that being a Woman of Destiny means that your Purpose will preserve you and keep you, protect you and sustain you even in the coldest alley, the harshest backyard, the darkest pit, the most evil abyss, the tightest shackles and the highest gallows until you fulfil that Purpose and enter your Destiny. Understand the power of your Destiny to pull you out of every place of wounding.

Fourthly, your Purpose and Destiny will give you an eagle's storm surviving skills, an eagle's sharp eye to maintain your Vision, an eagle's strong talons to keep a firm grip on your Destiny, so that you will be stronger and more empowered as you come out from that pain and wounds.

Fifthly, the grace that is as amazing as it is abundant will uphold you even when the ugly pain and wounds of the past try to sneak up on you, and your fierce resolve to fulfil your call and Destiny will help you overcome every wound and turn every scar into a star.

Sixthly, you should use those scars to teach others how to avoid or survive such traumatic events.

Seventhly, you should use your scars as a strength and proof of your ability to survive any challenges that you encounter in your journey to Destiny.

There are at least **seven scars** arising from **seven wounds** that are most common in us as women of Destiny, namely the scars arising from the wounds of **abandonment**, the scars arising from the wounds of **loss,** the scars arising from the wounds of **shame**, the scars arising from the wounds of **poverty**, the scars arising from the wounds of **abuse**, the scars arising from the wounds of **gross-injustice** and the scars arising from the wounds of **betrayal.**

1. FROM THE COLD ALLEYS OF ABANDONMENT TO THE HIGHWAY OF ACCEPTANCE

"As I look back on my life, I realize that every time I thought I was being rejected from something good, I was actually being redirected to something better." ~ Dr. Steve Maraboli.

Scars of abandonment threaten to make you abandon your Destiny.

a. Acknowledging Your Wounds of Abandonment

Abandonment is where people who are important to you, relinquish interest and responsibility over you.

Abandonment is a voluntary leaving of a person to whom one is bound by a special relation e.g. A wife, husband or child etc. it is to dessert someone by cutting connections, contact and communication etc.

Abandonment can either be **physical** (the actual separating from), **emotional** (withholding affection, love, intimacy and companionship), **spiritual** (withholding fellowship, prayer cover and spiritual nurturing and guidance), **financial** (withholding provision in the form material resources), **medical** (withholding treatment or access to treatment, medical facilities or medication), **social** (withholding friendship, moral support) etc.

"They say that abandonment is a wound that never heals. I say only that an abandoned child never forgets." ~ Mario Balotelli

The most common types of abandonment include;

- **Parental abandonment** like parents neglecting their parental role, care and love. When as a child you were not listened to or understood or nurtured in your areas of gifting or not appreciated, valued and accepted or where you felt no affection or attachment.

Psalms 27:10 *"When my father and mother forsake me, then the Lord will take care of me."*

- **Spousal or marital abandonment** - this is where a spouse leaves the other spouse either by physically deserting e.g., Separation or divorce or by remaining physically present but becoming emotionally unavailable.

- **Social abandonment** – this is where your friends abandon you and cut you from your social circle, or where a society or community ostracize you and make you an outcast for whatever reason.

- **Spiritual abandonment** – this is where you are excommunicated from your place of worship for whatever reason.

- **Political abandonment** – this is where citizens are abandoned by their government for whatever reasons and under whatever circumstances.

"Those who were supposed to protect me were the people who hurt me." ~ **Sylvester McNutt.**

Abandonment can also come in the form of being **"dropped"** by people who you trusted to have your back and in the process of being **"dropped"** you become crippled and lame and you ended up being hidden and isolated because of the shame you represent and you become side-lined, ignored and written-off.

Memories of being **"dropped"** could either be where a spiritual mentor or Destiny midwife neglects to nurture you or carelessly or knowingly causes you harm by **"cutting"** you instead of carefully **"circumcising"** you.

It could be where you are removed or down-graded, from a position of influence or unfairly sacked from a lucrative employment where you worked so hard and sacrificed so much or ejected from a business empire where you invested so much. It could also include where you were cut out from a significant social group, team or circle or even isolated from the family for whatever reasons.

Abandonment under any of these circumstances can really rock and shake your self-esteem and self-confidence and seriously erode your identity and hinder you from focusing on your Calling and Destiny.

The important thing is to ensure that we never become the abandoners by checking ourselves regularly and sincerely.

Your wounds of abandonment may have led to loss of identity, and an identity crisis, low self-esteem, low self-worth, guilt and shame, intense fear, flawed thinking, false beliefs, and impaired behaviours, which you will have to acknowledge, confront and overcome to enable you fulfil your Purpose and Destiny.

Do not abandon your identity because of your wounds of abandonment. ~ Unknown

b.   Tracing the effects of Abandonment

Abandonment comes with humiliation which may lead to offense bitterness and anger at those who **"dropped"** you. Like all forms of neglect, it leads to deep scaring, even though perhaps parental and spousal abandonment take the cup and leave the deepest scars.

In addition, abandonment has a way of impacting future relationships when the wound is not dealt with, because abandonment leads to mistrust, feelings of insecurity thereby hindering your ability to form healthy relationships. It also leads to constantly penalizing your current relationships due to your past pain from previous relationships.

Beware of repeating the cycle of abandonment. It is often said that people who suffered abandonment as children may be more likely to repeat this pattern with their own children or loved ones. So, you must recognize this pattern, so that you can break the "cycle of abandonment," because it can be very subtle and it may take you years to actually realize how you may be abandoning your own children or loved ones. This is because you cannot possibly imagine yourself doing so, considering how you suffered from it, and you may be blinded to it, because you probably do it subconsciously and unknowingly.

Also, your fear of future abandonment, can impact an otherwise healthy relationship, because you may subconsciously work to keep people from leaving you, by pouring hard work and effort into the relationship, then you might worry that they do not appreciate or reciprocate your efforts and end up being a people pleaser. If you don't deal with this fear of abandonment, eventually those people who had no intentions of leaving will leave because of your irrational behaviour.

Do not let your fear of future abandonment chase away someone who had no intention of leaving you

You may also be prone to long-term depression, often based on the fear that abandonment will recur which may cause you years of depression. The fear of abandonment impairs your ability to trust others, and it may make it harder for you to feel worthy or be intimate.

Fear of abandonment can literally affect your ability to live a meaningful productive life so that you fail to fulfil your Purpose and Destiny.

This kind of abandonment and isolation denies you certain privileges, denies you healthy social interaction and the ability to be economically productive. You remain in uncertainty and fear that you will die at that place of isolation and lameness, incapacitated and unable to ever fulfil your Purpose and Destiny.

"Beware you do not miss the invitation to the kings table because of your Lodebar scars." Unknown

c. How to Heal from Your Wounds of Abandonment

Learn to sharpen your self-awareness to tune into yourself to pay attention to your feelings, by making a concerted effort to love yourself and to own your needs, and by learning emotional management skills, you can begin the process of accepting your own true value as a human being.

Put your energy and focus and immerse yourself into fulfilling your Calling and Destiny so that your mind and your time are fully occupied to prevent you from dwelling on those wounds.

Relationships are a key tool in enabling you to fulfil your Purpose and Destiny and so your inability to develop and maintain healthy valuable Destiny relationships due to scars of abandonment may inevitably lead to an abortion of your Purpose.

Another way of healing is by addressing your abandoner where possible and sharing the pain and wounds that he or she caused, to enable you release any toxic emotions and thereby intentionally forgive those persons.

Your ability to become sensitive and empathetic to others who have suffered the same abandonment as you by offering loving support is another process of securing and accelerating your own healing.

Beware of the crippling effect of the wounds of abandonment. Understand your identity namely what defines you and what does not define, learn to forgive yourself and those that wounded you, learn to rebuild trust in people instead of generalizing that all people cannot be trusted.

Beware of ignoring the people around you by chasing those who have left you.

Be open to receive love and acceptance from others, so that you focus your energy on those positive relationships and remove your focus from those who abandoned you.

Know and believe that you did not cause the abandonment and that those who abandoned you may have been suffering from their own weaknesses, dysfunctions etc.

One of the key factors that will enable you to come out of your pain is to adopt a radical faith that no matter how abandoned you were, somehow you must arise from your lameness and limitations and embark on fulfilling your Destiny. So, you must adopt such a proactive mind-set and rise above your negative circumstances. Somehow, help is there to take you away from that cold alley of abandonment to the table of acceptance, adoption and a place where you are cherished, valued and protected.

You must remain emotionally strong and ensure that you don't harbour any toxic emotions like resentment, offense, bitterness and anger. Those toxic emotions will hold you captive and make you unable to move past your pain and woundedness. So, beware that toxic emotions or negative mind-set do not hinder you from seeing, discerning and sensing any help that may come your way because you might be too blinded or hardened and thereby miss your hour of visitation and doors of opportunity, when the time comes.

d. Learn how to spin your scars into stars

Turn this "scar of abandonment" into a "star of acceptance" and accept that you matter, especially by accepting that God who created you, loves you with an everlasting love and will never leave or forsake you.

Record your experiences, how you survived and healed from abandonment and the lessons you came out with and use it to help others.

Your scar could spin into a star and you may find yourself sitting and eating at the kings table clothed with favour and honour to the surprise of many who had written you off, and those who had dropped you and left you at "Lodebar", which symbolizes a place of lameness or of no word or communication but only isolation. (2 Samuel 9)

Beware you do not miss the invitation to the kings table because of your Lodebar wounds.

For sure, help will come at a time you least expect it and suddenly overnight you can be plucked out of Lodebar and placed at the king's table. Your Destiny will not give up on you and it will continue to seek you out and to break every limitation around you.

The power of the greatness within you, will lift you out of Lodebar just like the power of that greatness will strengthen you to leave your garden of "Gethsemane" and lift you to your "cross of Calvary" to fulfil that Destiny.

At the "kings table" your scars will be spined into stars and your significance, privileges, influence, power etc. will be restored overnight so as to enable and empower you to go on to fulfil your Destiny.

Let your scars of abandonment spin into stars of acceptance, and become known not as one who was abandoned but as one who is accepted and cherished and one who accepts and cherishes others affectionately.

2. FROM THE DEEP LAKE OF LOSS TO THE LANDSCAPE OF LIFE

"Grief is like living two lives. One is when you pretend everything is alright and the other is where your heart silently screams out in pain." ~ Unknown

The wounds of Loss threaten to abort and kill your Destiny.

a. Acknowledging Your Loss

Wounds of loss may symbolize loss by death of a loved one, loss of valued relationships, loss of treasured ties and bonds that are irreplaceable. This may destabilize you in many ways and you may not be able to cope with daily life. It could also mean loss of connections with the departed, their role in your life, like the loss of a father, or mother thus feelings of insecurity and disorientation etc.

Wounds of loss could also mean the breakdown and ending of other valuable relationships due to a number of reasons e.g., a divorce, a business partnership, a professional alliance or even a social network.

It could also entail the deprivation of property and assets, whether justifiable or not, or the loss of access or use of those properties and assets. It could also mean loss of lucrative positions of power and influence or even the loss of certain privileges and benefits.

Suffice that the loss is significant enough to cause severe pain and deep wounds whether as a result of the regret you feel for being responsible for that loss or the anguish you feel at the injustice caused to you by others.

Your wounds of loss through death of a loved one can be extremely painful depending on the cause of death e.g., suicide, murder, fatal accident, prolonged sickness.

Even though no death is without pain, when it is clearly premature (as opposed to resting from at a ripe old age) or where you had unresolved issues with the departed loved one, then the intensity will differ from one situation to another, and also because the impact of loss is determined by how close a relationship and bond one had with the deceased.

Some other painful losses that most women describe as worse than death, are for example divorce where a Woman did not see it coming because according to her there was nothing wrong with the marriage and she had no idea that there was a storm brewing right in front of her.

Where the husband disappears without any trace either through abduction or where he willingly seeks to hide and change his identity and disappear usually due to debts or whatever other reason without any regards as to the devastation, he causes the family. Another loss is where a child is stolen either on giving birth at the hospital or later on by child traffickers etc. which can be worse than loss by death.

Sometimes these kinds of losses where there is no closure because you are tormented by the thought that your lost loved one could be somewhere around only you cannot access them. Such a loss can literally paralyze you and bring you to a standard still.

Even though you must not deny your losses, you should not allow them to define you but instead allow those losses to teach you valuable lessons.

"Mostly it is loss which teaches us about the worth of things."
Arthur Schopenhauer

b. Tracing the effects of loss

Loss can cause you to lose the zeal passion and enthusiasm for life and deter your dreams, goals or even stagnate your life, depending on how you handle your grief and whether there is an adequate support system or not.

Of all losses, perhaps the loss through death is the most wounding because it can cause self-blame and guilt in cases where you feel you could have done something to save the life of your loved one and didn't do enough. The feelings of remorse and regret, can be overwhelming and the thought of "if only I had done this or that" I could have saved my loved one or where in a case of suicide you feel that something you said or did caused it.

"The loss is immeasurable but so is the love left behind." Unknown

Certain types of death may be particularly difficult to process, like losing a young child or baby may provoke feelings of anger and injustice because he or she didn't even have a chance to live. Where it is a suicide, you may be angry and feel that your loved one was extremely selfish in choosing that option and it may take you a long time to forgive that person. Where it is an unjustifiable death by murder or manslaughter, your anger towards those who caused it, can build up and keep you in a bondage pursuing illusive justice. Suffice to say that your attitude and response to these situations will determine your ability to heal and move on.

Loss can also lead to prolonged anger towards life where for instance you fail to understand why your loved one didn't heal. So, you keep your anger hidden inside and you may even convince yourself that you are not angry.

Suppressing your emotions of grief could also prolong the healing process, thus paralyzing and incapacitating you, jeopardizing your ability to fulfil your Purpose and Destiny.

With regard to loss of a child, tragically some couples are often unable to share their grief when they lose a child through death or where the child is stolen and many end up separating and divorcing to deal with their pain separately.

c. Healing from wounds of loss

To conquer "wounds of loss" you need to acknowledge your pain, anger, frustrations, depression, regret and guilt etc. and realize that grief can trigger many different and unexpected emotions and therefore be prepared to manage and handle those emotions.

You also need to understand that your grieving process will be unique to you so don't expect to grief same way as those around you because each person is unique in how they handle grief and loss. This is where strong and Destiny relationships, sincere social networks and a caring home church come in handy in supporting and walking this grief season with you.

"Grief is not a disorder, a disease or a sign of weakness. It is an emotional, physical and spiritual necessity, the price you pay for love. The only cure for grief is to grieve." ~ **Earl Grollman**

The responsibility upon you to fulfil your Purpose and Destiny does not become waived, suspended or cancelled just because you have been orphaned, widowed or suffered any other kind of loss. So, you must resolve and purpose to heal from your wounds of loss and forge on to your Destiny by prioritizing your Destiny above your pain and wounds, otherwise you'll end up increasing your loss by also losing your Destiny as well.

Your wounds and scars of loss should not torment or hinder you from loving again and forming new relationships especially where your loss was a spouse or child. These scars should not keep you dwelling on the loss, instead you must arise and love again and nurture again, at an even deeper intensity, so that your scars of loss spin into stars of love, and you defeat the power of that loss.

"Little by little we let go of loss but not of love." ~ *Unknown*

d. **Learn to spin your scars into stars**

As you continue to fulfil your Purpose and Destiny, you will be known and remembered not as the one who lost tragically but rather as the one who loved greatly, so let your scars of loss spin into stars and turn your lake of loss into a landscape of life.

Discern and glean out the lessons from each loss and use those lessons to transform your perceptions and paradigms where they were skewed and to teach others to survive and thrive after those losses.

Where the loss was of loved ones then you will learn to cherish those of your loved ones who have remained alive. You have learnt that none of us will live forever, so each day with our loved ones is precious. If the loss was in respect of broken relationships, then you will learn that in future you should guard and nurture your relationships. If the loss was in respect of property and assets then you will learn that in future you should be a good steward of that which is entrusted to you. If the loss was in respect of powerful positions of influence, then you will learn that in future you should fulfil the Purpose for which you were put in those powerful positions of influence.

Despite anything or anyone you may lose in your life, as long as you have not lost your Calling and Destiny, then that should be the motivation for your healing, so that you can move on to fulfil that Calling and Destiny.

3. FROM THE SHACKLES OF SHAME TO THE HALLS OF HONOUR

"Shame should be reserved for the things we choose to do, not the circumstances that life puts on us." ~ Ann Patchett

Wounds of Shame threaten to smoother your Destiny into silence.

a. Acknowledging your wounds of shame

Your shame could manifest feelings of mixed regret, self-blame, guilt. Self-hate, self-pity and dishonour either because you have defied and gone against the norms of your society, cultural standards and expectations (and whereby perhaps you may have become an outcast or an untouchable) or where you have done things you are personally ashamed of whether recklessly, or just out of poor choices.

For some women shame may arise where after a long relationship (which you were sure would end up in marriage) ends up as a broken engagement or even where you reach the altar, but you are left at the altar, devastated, because of the emotional and other investment that you have made into that relationship. Sometimes it could be that you are caught up in a scandal such as an illicit love affair, or embezzlement of funds in an organization or institution from where you limb away in shame.

Your wounds of shame could also have been caused by failure to achieve and accomplish expected goals or dreams. It could also be loss of a lucrative opportunity, position of prestige, power etc. due to discrimination, gender bias or victimization, or due to some wrong choices on your part whereby you become labelled as a failure or loser.

Maybe there are still people in your life who reinforce your shame? It might be your parents who continue to say and do things to control, belittle, or hurt you, or toxic friends and an insecure spouse who thinks, he can become secure by shaming you into insecurity.

Rejection can also bring about immerse sense of shame due to the feelings of worthlessness, repeated failure, or a series of traumatic events in your life that you felt helpless to control.

Beware because your shame can take you further than you want to go.

Shame is one of the worst emotions, because it is the feeling that there is something basically wrong with you, so that instead of seeing it as a result of the hate of others, you tragically blame yourself. This leads to self- hate because shame comes from the belief that, "I am basically flawed, inadequate, wrong, bad, unimportant, undeserving or not good enough". So, you seek to isolate and hide yourself because it's like a failure to meet your own ideals or standards.

Given that shame can lead you to feel as though your whole self is flawed, bad and deserving of rejection, it therefore causes you to hide or do something to save face, which leads to avoidance, which can lead to withdrawal or to addictions that attempt to block out and to mask the feelings of shame within you.

b.   Tracing the effects of shame.

Where you suffered sexual abuse as a child, it may become a cause of shame in your adulthood, especially where you feel embarrassed about your experience. Sadly, some abusive families cruelly impose the shame on you (the victim) for having been abused when you call the abuse what it is, or worse still they put the blame on you which is like adding salt to your wounds.

Irrespective of what caused your feelings and wounds of shame suffice to say it can have a very prejudicial effect on your identity and in your ability to fulfil your Purpose and Destiny because regardless of the triggers, when shame is experienced the deterioration of an esteemed sense of self can be devastating.

In addition to the typical emotions that can accompany shame, such as anger, rage, and anxiety, we can also include sadness, depression, depletion, loneliness, and emptiness as a result, yet these are the exact opposite elements you need to fulfil your Purpose and Destiny.

Tragically wounds of shame could also be formed where as a child you were physically abandoned, abused, or neglected. You often take on the shame that belongs to the adult who left or hurt you by assuming that it's because you were to blame. You must offload this false burden and let it return where it belongs in order for you to heal.

"You did not have the ability to stop what was done to you but you have the power to choose how to overcome them." ~ Unknown

c. Healing From Wounds of Shame

To overcome wounds of shame you may have to revisit your childhood; as painful as this might be, it's important to have a realistic understanding that shame is not your fault. Visiting the root cause of the shame is the first step to healing and overcoming those wounds of shame.

When dealing with wounds of shame always recognize your triggers and start to notice what triggers your feelings of shame. This may be difficult at first as we often bury our feelings under layers of makeup and perfume and designer wear, but instead confide in your trusted relationships and Destiny helpers.

"If we share our stories with someone who responds with empathy and understanding, shame can't survive." ~ Brene Brown.

To overcome the wounds of shame, practice self- compassion and forgiveness when you feel ashamed, it's hard to be kind and loving towards yourself, but you can practice self-compassion even before you really feel, it by confessing it.

Challenge your negative thoughts which often trigger shameful feelings. When you mentally revisit conversations or situations where you felt shamed or if your thoughts are a series of self-criticisms, you are only strengthening your shame, so stop and shame your shame.

d. **Learn to Spin Your Scars of Shame into Stars of Honour**

Stand up to your wounds of shame, tame them and defame them into eternal silence, because to fulfil Purpose and Destiny, you must possess a very secure identity.

Spin your scars of shame into stars of affirmation and your shackles of shame into songs of self-love and honour instead of being called the shameful Woman, call yourself the affirmed Woman.

Purpose to use the power in the valuable lessons that you learn from these scars of shame to propel you to your Destiny.

4. FROM THE ABYSS OF ABUSE TO THE ARMCHAIR OF AFFIRMATION

"There is no timestamp on trauma. There isn't a formula that you can insert yourself into to get from horror to being healed. Be patient, take your space. Let your journey to the balm." ~Dawn Serra

Wounds of Abuse threaten to throw your Destiny into oblivion.

a. **Acknowledging your abuse**

Abuse comes in different shades and shapes such as physical, verbal, emotional, mental, financial, sexual, social and spiritual etc. and you may have suffered from one or more of the various types of abuse during your childhood or later in adulthood or even currently, which left you with deep and painful wounds that threaten to paralyze you and hinder you from fulfilling your Purpose and Destiny.

"It is not the bruises of the body that hurts. It is the wounds of the heart and the scars on the mind." ~ Aisha Mizra

In the Bible we find two Women both called Tamar, who suffered abuse albeit in different circumstances (Genesis 38 and 2 Samuel 13)

The "Tamar trauma" syndrome refers to the gross injustices, discrimination, and abuse by your own family and loved ones (whether it is physical, emotional, social, mental, financial, spiritual or relational).

The "Tamar trauma" is where you are short changed into a life of shame, humiliation, and embarrassment, due to no fault of your own.

Perhaps what makes the "Tamar trauma" so deep and regrettable is because the pain is caused by those who have an inherent duty, obligation and responsibility to love and protect you.

A "Tamar trauma" is often as a result of your innocence and naivety when you trust before you test and it is as a result of those nearest and dearest to you, having a sick and warped sense of entitlement as regards your life and believing that they can treat you whichever way they want to, and get away with it.

A "Tamar trauma" is also as a result of you having no power, no right, and no voice to dictate your own Destiny because you are under the care and responsibility of your family or a society that is oppressive.

b. **Tracing the effects of abuse**

The irony about a "Tamar trauma" is that often you may even be in a very privileged position, where you ought to have the necessary power and leverage but you don't due to defective systems of discrimination and oppression against Women which leaves you voiceless and helpless and unable to defend yourself from prejudice and harm.

Perhaps what makes the pain greater is the failure by those who have the power and responsibility to punish your abuser but they fail to do so, thereby releasing your abuser from the consequences of his actions.

This injustice is perhaps what deepens your wounds and causes a spirit of rejection within you, feelings of worthlessness and low self-esteem etc.

A "Tamar trauma" leaves you in profound grief and suffering because beyond the pain of the abuse is the greater and deeper pain of the indifference and lack of compassion and remorse by your abuser.

A "Tamar trauma" also has the effects of ostracizing you and isolating you as an outcast whereby the culture and traditions judge you harshly for something abominable that was done to you by no fault of your own.

A "Tamar trauma" seriously prejudices your Destiny because it cripples and paralyses you threatening to bury you in that place where you encountered that pain and wounds.

c. Healing from the wounds of abuse

Your trauma is not your fault, but your healing is your responsibility

Notwithstanding and without in any way belittling the devastation and impact that abuse may have had on you, having a revelation that you are a vessel of Destiny is perhaps the greatest motivation in helping you to heal from that abuse. You must climb out of whatever abyss it has thrown you into, and dive into the wells of wellness because for every abyss of abuse there is definitely a well of wellness.

You must choose to see that it is your abusers and those reluctant to punish them, who are dysfunctional and that it is not your fault. You must choose your response towards your abusers very carefully, because it is often not what is done to you, but it is your choice of response, that has the most impact on you.

Lk.6:28 – *"Bless those who curse you, and pray for those who spitefully use you."*

Climb out of your Abyss of abuse and immense yourself in the wells of wellness.

So irrespective of the type of abuse, you should start by identifying **who** abused you, (i.e., trusted and close loved ones or strangers), **where** you were abused, (was it within your family home or an institution) in **which** way you were abused.

Understanding the factors that led to the abuse, acknowledging the effects the abuse has had on you and most importantly addressing and confronting that abuse and the wounds of that abuse, will help heal you from those wounds.

d. Learn to turn your scars of abuse into stars of care.

Do not allow your Tamar Trauma to define you.

You must never allow your **"Tamar trauma"** to define you, or distort your identity or erode your security in who you were born to be and what you were created to do.

You must get up from where you suffered and endured your abuse and you must purpose to bury that past in order to arise and build your future. You must become a radical voice that stands and speaks against all forms of abuse, discrimination and disempowerment.

Let your scars of abuse spin into stars of affirmation and turn your abyss of abuse into a chamber of care and instead of being known as the one who was abused, be known as the one who cares and cherishes others.

5. FROM THE GALLOWS OF GROSS INJUSTICE TO THE GATES OF EQUITY

Scars of Gross-injustice threaten to lock up your potential for your Destiny.

a. Acknowledging your wounds of injustice

What is Your Gross Gallow of Injustice?

One of the most aggravated insults and assaults is the blatant, grievously wicked actions and practices where, you are so grossly and unjustly treated in situations where you are so sincerely innocent and you undergo such severe suffering, pain and irreplaceable loss, that your life is literally turned upside down overnight.

Maybe you were maliciously or recklessly falsely accused of crimes and wrongs you never committed possibly due to mistaken identity to by wicked devices of people out to destroy you for whatever reasons and you end up in the "prison of false accusation" for years.

You or your loved one may have been denied your basic human rights to access certain needs like medical treatment, and you end up developing a terminal health condition that could have been prevented and now you are a pale shadow of yourself, incapacitated.

Or where your loved ones like spouses, parent or children are taken away from you without any justifiable cause and you are left bleeding emotionally and fighting a mental breakdown because it's like a part of you was cut off.

Or was it a reckless insensitive false reporting by the media that took your name and your reputation and thrashed it so mercilessly, you cannot even walk down a street for the shame and scandal.

Sometimes it is your hard-earned wealth and substance that you have laboured for honestly and diligently for years so as to leave an inheritance for your children's children (as the bible says) but overnight it is viciously grabbed from you through a hideous corrupt judiciary that has shamelessly chosen to sell justice to the highest bidder, leaving you desolate and impoverished.

Sometimes those responsible for your gross injustice did so arrogantly just because they had the position and power or money to do so, like a government regime that wields arbitrary and dictatorial power.

It could be a spouse whose money robbed and tore away your helpless infants from your breast. It could be a financial institution with the monopoly to hold you hostage as it breaches every rule in the book or an unscrupulous opportunist who accuses you of unspeakable acts of immorality because you rejected their evil advances. Sometimes someone somewhere is jealous of you and the greatness and influence within you, so they seek to destroy you.

b. Tracing the effects of gross injustice

Gross injustice can leave deeply painful wounds because of the ruined and stolen lives or damaged families, who were emotionally ripped apart. The body bound up in infirmity. The reputation that had taken so long to build and one minute to destroy. Not to mention, the isolation and alienation from your people and community who may shun you because they believed the lies and fabrications.

Your pain and anguish can affect every area of your life. Physically due to sickness, emotionally, due to toxic, bitter emotions that hold you captive, mentally because of the stress, socially, because of the isolation, financially and also spiritually because you may reach a point where you misdirect your anger in the wrong direction or to the wrong people or blame life for dealing you a bad hand.

c. **Learn to heal from wounds of gross injustice**

Some of the most powerful and effective ways of healing from these scars of injustice are:

Firstly, choose your Destiny over anger, pain, revenge and vindication. Once you cast a very clear vote for your Destiny using your power of choice, then your Destiny will choose you and it will follow you to prison (whether it be a physical or emotional prison) and wherever else your gross injustice will drag you. Your Purpose will preserve and keep you alive, and finally release you from that prison.

Secondly, keep your focus on your Destiny instead of focusing on the hateful ugly face of gross injustice. Continue to do whatever is within your ability to do feed your Purpose and Destiny, despite your hard and harsh circumstances. Gradually the hateful ugly face of gross injustice will dim from your mind, heart and soul and your Purpose and Destiny will become magnified to overshadow that gross injustice.

Thirdly, you must develop such an intense and radical hatred for anything that even has the slightest smell and appearance of gross injustice, and be transformed into such a passionate, guardian of justice and fairness.

d. Learn to spin your scars of gross injustice into stars

Turn Your Gallows of Gross-Injustice into Gates of Liberty.

Let your scars of gross-injustice spin into stars of fairness and **justice** and turning your gallows of gross-injustice into gates of justice.

6. FROM THE PITS OF POVERTY TO THE MINES OF ABUNDANCE

Scars of poverty threaten to cut off vital resources from your Destiny.

"Poverty is not just a lack of money; it is not having the capacity to realise one's full potential as a human being." ~ Amartya Sen

a. Acknowledging your wounds of poverty

Just How Deep Was Your Pit of Lack?

These wounds may be because you lived your entire childhood (or even beyond your childhood) in such abject poverty and lack, in a continuous state of not having enough material substance, possessions or income for your most basic needs like food, shelter, clothing medical etc.

Maybe you learnt to endure groaning hunger pangs daily, crippling fear, anxiety and insecurity because shelter was often temporary without any guarantee, leaving you exposed to the harsh elements and lurking dangers of rape and violence etc.

without any proper sanitation, clean water, or where health care and even basic education was almost inaccessible or intermittent.

"Poverty is the worst form of violence." ~ Mahatma Gandhi

b. Tracing the effects of the wounds of poverty

Those barren years of powerlessness and lack can leave you with very deep wounds and scars, because of the pain, anger and bitterness of feeling like a second-class human or a child of a lesser God, who was dealt a very bad hand without any explanation as to why you were the one cruelly selected for such a harsh reality.

Your pain may have been compounded when you saw other children around you living in scandalous abundance without any evidence of what they might have done to be so advantaged.

"Poverty is not an accident. Like slavery or apartheid, it is man-made and can be removed by actions of human beings." ~ **Nelson Mandela.**

Severe poverty and extreme lack leaves you in powerlessness with a lack of freedom and choices that will force you to settle for and accept some sufferings that no human should have to, like abusive relationships, cruel enslavement and exploitation.

This dark pit of poverty can understandably lead to strong and negative emotions of anger directed at whoever you may perceive as being responsible for your desperate state, whether it be God, the Government etc. You may develop a deep resentment towards people who are well off and a critical judgment spirit as to how and where they got their resources, terming them either thieves corrupt or devil worshippers as you seek to soothe your pain.

Your ability to relate to and engage with valuable lucrative relationships (business networks, strategic alliances and beneficial collaborations) becomes seriously hampered by your resentment and your past financial pain. Your critical and judgmental opinion of the wealthy can get in the way causing you to behave badly and bitterly. You may abort any potential breakthrough and financial empowerment. So, you must stop this resentment in order to heal.

Having being so destitute and impoverished, can also give rise to deep bitterness because you suffered health problems that left you with long term negative effects, that limit you one way or another or you missed a proper education to equip you and give you a fighting chance among your peers. The inevitable social ills that come with being poverty stricken (because of the undesirable environment) can also wound you deeply.

Maybe that poverty led and forced you to do things to survive (like criminal acts or prostitution etc.) that contradicted your moral code and degraded you and left you wounded and stigmatized.

The tragic thing about the wounds of poverty and lack is that even when you finally begin to climb out of that pit of poverty (by your hard work and God's grace) and you begin to build and create your own wealth. There may be traces of woundedness that hinder you from enjoying your wealth.

The wounds from the pain, anger, jealousy, resentment and bitterness you had developed in your dark years of poverty keep rearing their ugly scabs, threatening to derail you from your Purpose and Destiny.

The unfortunate consequence of these unhealed wounds is that they torment you with your past financial pain and other toxic emotions which blind you and manifest in many shocking ways.

c. Healing from the wounds of poverty

Your bitterness and anger makes you develop an arrogant, independent, self- sufficient ego, whereby you are obsessed with proving yourself and making it on your own without anybody's help. This "one Woman show" and solo program, leads to failure, because wealth creation requires relationships and networks. So, heal this wound by uprooting this bitterness.

Do not fear poverty, let poverty fear you.

Your past fear of poverty and lack, left you hardened and your unhealthy vow that you will never lack again, means that your pursuit of wealth is based on wrong motivation and it becomes an unhealthy obsession that drives you into creating wealth by whatever means.

This opens dangerous doors in suspect dealings, compromises and breach of ethics thereby defiling your wealth (as ill-gotten gain which you can lose any time). So, healing this wound will require you to change your perspective and motivation as to why you create wealth and ensure that you do so to fulfil your Purpose and Destiny.

When pain of poverty spills all over.

Having been poor physically could make you "poor" in other areas of your life like "poor mind-set" that thinks small for lack of capacity to visualize big dreams and Visions also a "poor heart" unable to love and feel deeply and sincerely and a "poor hand" that is stingy and not generous to giving and sharing.

"Overcoming poverty is not a gesture of charity, it is an act of justice." ~ Nelson Mandela

So, as you seek to prosper physically, you must also seek to prosper the other areas of your life in order to heal this wound of poverty.

d. **Learn to spin your scars of poverty into stars**

Therefore, spin your scars of poverty and lack into stars of plenty by making your pit of poverty into a mountain of abundance, and become defined not as the one who was poverty stricken but as the Woman who is creating wealth for a Purpose.

Let your scars of poverty spin into stars of plenty and turn your pit of poverty into a mountain of abundance and prosperity with a Purpose.

7. FROM THE BACKYARD OF BETRAYAL TO THE LOUNGE OF LOYALTY

"When someone betrays you, it is a reflection of their character, not yours." ~ Unknown

Scars of betrayal threaten to push your Destiny into a neglected place.

a. **Acknowledging wounds of betrayal**

(The Place of Betrayal)

Often in your journey to Destiny, you will be betrayed by the very people that you are nurturing, empowering and sacrificing for and often those people are the ones from your own internal circle so it is even more painful than if it had been betrayal by outsiders and strangers.

"The saddest thing about betrayal is that it never comes from your enemies." Unknown

When you come to that **place of betrayal,** the emotions you might experience may be disbelief, shock, intense pain, regret, anger, bitterness and resentment, feeling violated and abused because you feel that you have been taken advantage of and taken for a fool.

"Sometimes the person who you would take a bullet for is the person behind the trigger." ~ Taylor Swift

Learn to test your trust.

Betrayal will either be in a situation where you have trusted certain people and entrusted confidential and sensitive74 information or documents but those people break that trust by disclosing and diverging that confidential and sensitive information (whether they do it knowing or unknowingly maliciously or out of recklessness). The result is that they have broken the trust you had in them and their actions end up harming and prejudicing you.

Another situation is where you may expose yourself and become vulnerable with someone and show your weaknesses, failings and shortcomings or even reveal your mistakes and wrongful actions and that person proceeds to betray you by taking advantage and using that knowledge to either blackmail you, shame you or embarrass you and worst of all put you into trouble with your authorities.

"Each betrayal begins with trust." ~ Martin Luther

Sometimes it is where in a relationship your spouse becomes unfaithful, contrary to the vows and commitments you have made to one another or where those who are supposed to take care of you abandon or abuse you in one way or another.

In a workplace situation, someone may 'throw you under the bus', by shifting blame on you and making you liable for something you are not.

"The saddest thing about betrayal is that it doesn't come from your enemies." ~ Unknown

b. Tracing the effects of betrayal

Whatever kind of betrayal you encounter, suffice to say it has the effect of making you fearful to ever trust again or sacrifice for people again or to even love again which may take you years to overcome and heal from, because of the wounds it causes in you that are deep and painful.

Betrayal can also paralyze you and keep you stagnant at the place of betrayal, hindering you from moving on in the fulfilment of your Purpose and Destiny, thereby prejudicing you.

c. Healing from wounds of betrayal

Betraying your betrayal by throwing it under the bus

It is therefore important to make a deliberate choice to get up from your wounds of betrayal by:

Firstly, forgiving yourself, where you feel you were careless or negligent by putting yourself in a position where you could easily be betrayed or trusting people you had no business trusting. By taking responsibility for your own wrong choices that caused you to be betrayed.

Secondly, you must forgive those who betrayed you and let go of the pain, anger, and regret in order to move on.

Thirdly, you must remember that by remaining at the place of betrayal you are actually empowering the wrong doers and increasing the prejudice to yourself instead of arising and moving on.

After you have suffered all manner of betrayals (because indeed they will be many) and you have come to a place of healing then you will learn valuable lessons going forward.

You will come to a place of reconciliation in your heart and in your spirit and realize that fulfilling your Purpose and Destiny will not come with accolades and gratitude but nonetheless the absence of such will not stop you from continuing in your journey to Destiny.

"Don't be discouraged, it's often the last key in the bunch that opens the lock." ~ Unknown

d. Learn to turn your scars of betrayal into stars

Therefore, learn to spin your scars of betrayal into stars of loyalty by making your "backyard of betrayal" into a "lounge of loyalty". Remember that the scars of betrayal if not healed threaten to push your Purpose and Destiny to a neglected state and place. So, get up and move on.

One of the most powerful ways to heal from and defeat the wounds of betrayal is by intentionally choosing to trust again, because your Calling and Destiny will require you to continuously develop and maintain relationships and you cannot do so unless you learn to extend trust again.

"The knives of betrayal and drama cut deep and hurt… but they also trim away the nonsense and reveal your true friends." Steve **Maraboli**

Destiny Questions To Ponder On

1. What other **ways or measures** can one take to heal from the wounds of abandonment, loss, shame, abuse, gross-injustice, poverty and betrayal?

2. What are the other circumstances **examples** of abandonment, loss, shame, abuse, gross-injustice, poverty and betrayal?

3. What are the other **effects** of abandonment, loss, shame, abuse, gross-injustice, poverty and betrayal?

4. What are the other **ways** of spinning each of these scars into stars?

5. Which of these **wounds** have you personally suffered from, what were the circumstances, what measures did you take to heal and how have you used the scars from those wounds?

6. How would you go about **helping** another woman suffering from any of these wounds?

7. Do you know anyone either in the Bible or in history who aborted their Destiny because of an unhealed wound?

Chapter 4

THE PAIN PATTERNS OF A DESTINY CHAMPION

Projecting Your Pain Points Into Power Points

Chapter Preview

1. *What is your Salty Pillar – why are you cheating on your future with your past?*

2. *What is your Bendedness – what burdens have you allowed to weigh you down?*

3. *What are your Leaky Issues – what treasures are leaking out of you?*

4. *Your Thirsty Thirst – are you quenching your void and emptiness from the right wells?*

5. *Your Squinty Sight – are you allowing your outward appearance to undermine the fruitfulness within you?*

6. *Your Barrenness – are you focusing on what breaks your barrenness or on what mocks your barrenness?*

7. *Who short changed you? – are you willing to leave your isolation and come dine at the palace at the King's table?*

OPENING REMARK

"Never underestimate the pain of a person, because in all honesty, everyone is struggling. Some people are just better hiding it than others" ~ **Will Smith**

A pain point is a specific problem, affliction, agony, anguish, distress and torment that is acute, intense and concentrated, yet often so subtle that those around you may remain oblivious to your pain unless you speak of it.

"Holding back your tears and taking a smile telling people you are fine is the most painful thing." ~ **Unknown**

Every Woman passionate for her Destiny will encounter subtle struggles that will be deeply private and personal, so she may not be able to share this pain with too many people. She has to take full responsibility in victoriously overcoming it and turning it into a power point, that will equip and empower her in fulfilling her Call and Destiny.

All women either in the bible or in history who successfully went on to fulfil their Destiny and leave lasting legacies had one thing in common, namely they acknowledged their pain points as opposed to denying them, they sought to understand the meaning of their pain points, the root cause of those pain points, the devastating negative effects that those pain points had on their Destiny, and they then deliberately and purposely made radical Destiny choices that turned their pain points into their power points that then propelled them to their Destiny and taught them valuable lessons.

"When it hurts – observe. Life is trying to teach you something" ~ **Anita Krizzan**

These pain points are subtle, meaning that they are hidden deep within you and you may often even ignore them, but you must acknowledge them and fix them because even though subtle they are potent and can prejudice your Calling and Destiny.

Beware that you don't become your pain point and that your struggle does not define you because you are stronger than that pain point and struggle and it is your victory over it that should define you.

Remember that the same hot boiling water that softens a potato is the same hot water that hardens a boiled egg so it is about what you are made of that will uphold and sustain you and not your circumstances and afflictions.

Psalm 34:18 – *"The LORD is near to those who have a broken heart, and saves such as have a contrite spirit."*

Always remember that the struggles you are in now are building strength that you will need in the future, so learn to see your pain points as potential power points and embrace those struggles towards your healing.

"Struggling is not the identity, you must learn to live while you struggle, such that anyone who sees you can separate the struggle from your life." ~ Unknown

So don't get lost and stuck in the struggle that you refuse to be part of life, you must resolve to live your life even in the midst of all these subtle struggles and it is in doing so that you will accelerate your healing and victory.

1. WHAT IS YOUR SALTY PILLAR?

(Why are you cheating on your future with your past?)

a. **What Does the Pillar of Salt Symbolize?**

"You know you are on the right track when you become disinterested in looking back." Unknown

You cannot effectively progress to your future and Destiny, when your gaze and focus is still fixed on past things that you should have left behind because they are either not adding value or worse still, they were hindering your future and Destiny. Stop cheating on your future with your past.

The term **"pillar of salt"** is commonly used to symbolize an obsession with the past, whether it be pleasures, bad choices, desires, comforts, indulgences, toxic relationships, stale successes or dismal failures, unhealthy habits and behaviours, including soulish attachments to people, or places (whether physically or emotionally).

The word **"pillar"** symbolizes a strong supporting monument and the word "Salt" symbolizes purity, truth and preservation. The story in the bible where the term **"Pillar of Salt"** comes from (where a Woman known as **lots wife** become a pillar of salt because she looked back at a toxic place that she was supposed to be escaping from (**Genesis 19:26**)) is meant to be a lesson and warning to us that looking back instead of looking forward to the future will paralyze and stagnate us from fulfilling our Destiny.

b. **What has Caused You to Become a Pillar of Salt?**

You become a pillar of salt because of;

Lack of a single mind – this is where one season in your life comes to an end and you are unable or unwilling to fully or successfully transition and step into the next new season of your life. So, you get stuck in between seasons with one foot in the old season and one foot in the new season (transitional failure) which means that you are double minded, unable to make clear decisions and a procrastinator.

You will have different seasons in your life (either in your business, marriage, relationships, career, spiritual walk with God, health etc.) So, you must be able to discern when a particular season in any of those areas comes to an end and another one begins so that you step into the new season in that area.

For example, in your career, your season in a particular organization or institution may come to an end either so that you transition into another area of your career or you retire. The season for your young adult children to continue living with you comes to an end and they may need to transition into their own space as they mature and become self-reliant. The season of you being an employee may come to an end and you begin to transition into the season of being an employer or the season for your business changes from being a side hustle into becoming a bigger business enterprise.

- **Lack of vision** – where your desire for the future is not as strong as your desire for the past and therefore you are unable to visualize what lies ahead and you are bound by what is in the past.

- **Lack of sufficient revelation** – where you do not have an understanding of your Calling and the Destiny that lies ahead of you in the sense that you have not discovered it nor embarked on fulfilling it.

- **Lack of passion** – where as a result of not knowing your Purpose and Destiny, you do not have any passion or motivation towards it.

c.   How Does Your Pillar of Salt affect your Destiny?

As stated above, looking back definitely and negatively impacts on your ability to fulfil your Destiny; looking back can cost you precious and valuable time and opportunity which you should be employing for your future.

It weakens you emotionally and physically and drains valuable energy out of you that you should be investing in your future and Destiny. It also means that you cannot sufficiently focus on the present and the things you need to be doing towards your future and Destiny.

Constantly looking back at a toxic past is likely to cause you to contaminate and defile your present and your future. Hence the reason Lot's wife in the bible could not be allowed to step in the future while her gaze was still fixed on her toxic past.

Allowing yourself to be bound and burdened by baggage from your past means that, that past takes up valuable space in your life, yet you need to make room in your life for what lies ahead. The weights and heaviness of past baggage literally overwhelm and weigh you down, hindering you from making any meaningful progress towards your future and Destiny.

How to Dissolve Your Pillar of Salt

"Don't look back you are not going that way." ~ Mary Engelbreit

Your pillar of salt will dissolve when your gaze shifts and you choose your Destiny over your history.

If you are serious about fulfilling your Destiny, then you must purpose to deliberately and intentionally change and realign your focus from the past and towards your future.

In your journey to Destiny, you must constantly purpose to set your heart, mind and soul on things above and on things ahead that relate to your Destiny. Realize that in every situation there is a grace period within which you must do what you know you must, in order to avoid the danger and risk of aborting your Purpose and Destiny.

Destiny requires constant movement, actions, haste, and decisiveness. So, you must shake and dissolve yourself from being a pillar of salt and let go of all that you must, in order to lay hold of that which matters.

Your past, present and future life can be likened to a place and sometimes your place may need to burn down because of accumulated toxicity that is likely to contaminate you for where you are going.

The worst thing you can do is to turn back to your burning place to salvage any of those things there because in the process you may get burnt into ashes with no viable chance of ever fulfilling your Destiny. You cannot look back when you are disconnecting and being saved from a destructive place, person or whatever.

So, get over your past and dim all memories of your past pain, failure, etc. and do not lose your future by looking at your past because your past whether painful or joyful should only act as valuable lessons and as a motivation for you to chase your future and fulfil your Destiny.

Philippians 3:13 – Brethren, I do not count myself to have apprehended; but one thing I do, forgetting those things which are behind and reaching forward to those things which are ahead."

2. WHAT IS YOUR BENDEDNESS?

(What burdens have you allowed to weigh you down?)

"Few people are bent from hard work than are crooked from avoiding it." ~ ZigZiglar

a. What does Your Bendedness Symbolize?

In the physical, to be bent means that your body and back are not upright, usually caused by a problem in your posture, which may be due to muscle rigidity or a bent spine.

Symbolically the word "bent" is often used to mean that you are not straight, so you are crooked, which means that you are not honest, not upright and that there is an absence of integrity, transparency and accountability in certain or all areas of your life. The fact that your bendedness in the physical could be as a result of a spinal problem symbolizes that you may be one who lacks courage or you have a problem taking a stand on issues hence the phrase "she has no spine."

Being bent also says that you have some kind of disfigurement and crippling, that you are burdened, overwhelmed and oppressed or even ashamed because of your downward looking posture. It could also indicate a discouragement, despair or despondency…. "She walked away with her head bent."

Sometimes being bent over could also symbolize that you are easily taken advantage of by people overlooking you.

b. What is Causing Your Bendedness?

Your symbolic bendedness may be mental, emotional, physical, social, spiritual, financial etc. Perhaps you are bent because of oppression and attacks by your Destiny killers, shameful experiences, pain and failure, gross injustices, bitterness, anger, unforgiving, depression, fear, doubt etc.

Or perhaps you could have undergone financial distress and embarrassment, or sometimes it could be a scandal or a public smear on your reputation and character and social standing.

Suffice to say that whatever has caused your bendedness the enemy's scheme is to keep you down without a Vision of seeing your bright future and great Destiny because he knows that once you have no Vision you will perish, and your Destiny aborted.

Sometimes it could be that you are carrying "strange burdens" or "other people's monkeys" which have no value add for your Destiny. Or just burdens that you have no business carrying like past pain and baggage, worries and anxieties, wrong mind-sets and distorted perceptions.

Acknowledging your bendedness is a crucial step to your healing and confronting what caused your bendedness is the second step and the third step is to make a deliberate choice to straighten up in whatever area in your life.

c. How is Your Bendedness Affecting Your Destiny?

When you are physically bent you cannot lift your head and eyes to see up or forward which symbolizes that you lack foresight or a Vision for your future. It also symbolizes that you have no clear or full perception of what is head of you, to enable you plan for it or walk towards it.

Also, you cannot even see people in front of you fully so you cannot be able to sufficiently vet and form an correct opinion about your relationships. Consequently, your relationships are based on your limited understanding of those people's characters and qualities, their motives and agendas in your life and worse of all, you are not able to discern or assess whether or not they are adding value to your life or Destiny.

You can't even fully see opportunities, and open doors in front of you that are necessary for your Destiny (to enable you walk into them) and this denies you the capacity to make proper Destiny choices and decisions.

"One can't think crooked and walk straight." ~ Unknown

Perhaps the saddest thing is your inability to fully see and appreciate dangers and warnings in front of you so as to avoid them and another disadvantage of being bent is it suffocates your potential. Your "bendedness" is a limitation that doesn't allow your full potential to be unleashed nor your gifts, talents and skills to be fully utilized.

When you are bent over it means that you are lacking confidence and therefore have a low self-esteem and a low opinion of yourself which distorts and erodes your real identity and throws you into an identity crisis.

Therefore, your ability to discover and dedicate to your Purpose is greatly hindered and prejudiced. Being bent means you cannot effectively walk the journey to your Destiny.

d. Straighten Up from Your Bendedness

Your bendedness will end when your passion for your Purpose and Destiny becomes an obsession and your desire to see that Destiny makes you radically lift your eyes and head up.

Your "bendedness" is a bondage because it keeps you bound and disenabled, and you must detest it enough in order to get yourself straightened up and become upright and stand tall.

- The **first,** solution is to be loosed and released into your Destiny. Your loosing will require a radical shift of your mind-set, whereby you resolve to forgive yourself and others of anything that was either self-inflicted or others -inflicted that has made you bent.

  To disentangle and disconnect yourself totally whether physically or emotionally etc. from all the root causes of your bendedness, whether they be places, people, things, mind-sets and emotions.

- The **second** solution is to be offloaded of all the weight and baggage that has bent you over. This is where you will require strategic Destiny relationships and connections to help offload you of all that weight and baggage because you can't do it on your own.

  This is because your walk and journey to Destiny will require you to have key relationships like Destiny helpers in the form of mentors, ladders, burden bearers etc. who will stand with you in your season of "bendedness" but whose real value is in helping to straighten you up from your "bendedness" provided you are willing to be straightened.

- The **third** solution is that once you have been loosed and offloaded then you must straighten yourself up and get rid of everything that had got you crooked (such as dishonesty corruption, bribery, and lack of integrity, fakeness and falseness, strange burdens etc.) by making intentional choices, decisions and taking the corresponding actions radically and diligently.

Beware that some people around you may not want you to be healed of your bendedness and be straightened up. This is because of their own critical and judgmental attitudes whereby they believe that you are not entitled to the healing and straightening up (because of their legalistic doctrines. Others will argue that it is not the season for you to be healed and straightened up or you have not qualified to be healed and straightened up, because they also lack compassion and mercy.

In addition, those who were benefitting from your being bent may also not want your healing or straightening, especially where they were using you to operate crooked transactions and deals.

3. WHAT ARE YOUR LEAKY ISSUES?

(What Treasures are Leaking Out of You?)

"Pay mind to your own life, your own health and wholeness. A bleeding heart is of no help to anyone if it bleeds to death." ~ Frederick Buechner

a. What Does Your Leaking Issue Mean and Symbolize?

Sometimes in your journey to Destiny, you may encounter a subtle struggle in the form of "bleeding" that appears ceaseless and unending causing you a lot of trauma and hindering you from effectively fulfilling your Destiny. Your "bleeding" symbolizes some form of leakage or haemorrhaging whereby certain things whether good or bad are flowing out of you.

Your "bleeding" and leaking could be of a physical, emotional, financial, social, mental, or spiritual nature depending on what is leaking and flowing out of you. So, it is important to identify where bleeding is happening (in which area of your life) acknowledge it and resolve to address it.

Your "bleeding" can represent three perspectives.

- **Firstly,** the wasteful leaking of necessary and valuable things within you.
- **Secondly** the leaking of toxic unnecessary and destructive things within you (i.e., an **offensive** leaking, of things you are allowing to flow out of you in an offensive manner).
- **Thirdly** is where the leaking is acceptable and must happen in seasons and cycles to emit certain elements from within you, that must be removed in order to prepare you for fruitfulness i.e., a kind of purging or a pruning for growth.

Some "bleeding" normally comes out of the most private part of a Woman symbolizing that often you are suffering from a very private deep place (emotionally) which makes it very difficult for you to share your pain with others.

b. What Causes Your Leaking Issue?

i. The **first** kind of bleeding and leaking is whereby you are losing valuable and necessary things through that bleeding and leaking. This is either self-inflicted whereby due to your own wrong choices and actions you cause harm to yourself, or it is externally inflicted where harm is caused to you by other people due to their jealousy, envy or malice.

Irrespective of whether it is internal or external, suffice to say that a "puncturing" takes place and there is a bleeding and leaking in either or all of the following:

- **"Financial bleeding"** symbolically means that while you are generating, wealth, income and resources, you are nonetheless losing them either because of your own poor and negligent financial decisions and management, bad stewardship or as a result of other people sucking and siphoning that wealth and resources from you through deception and manipulation etc.

"Beware of a little expense; a small leak will sink a great ship." ~ **Benjamin Franklin**

- **"Social bleeding"** or leaking symbolically means that although you are identifying and connecting to valuable Destiny relationships, nonetheless you find yourself constantly loosing those valuable relationships because of some emotional or social dysfunction on your part where you are unable to manage your emotions properly. Or where you have not developed your self -awareness, social and people skills that would normally help you in maintaining healthy relationships.

- **"Spiritual bleeding"** symbolically means you are unable to retain the valuable teachings, lessons, from the word of God including even Visions and dreams that God may give you in communicating with you. Worst of all it could be your walk with God is unstable and you keep backsliding or falling short as you struggle with certain sins and weaknesses.

ii. The **second kind** of "bleeding" and leaking is (where, you allow toxic and negative things to flow out of you that are quite offensive to those around you), for example your words and your speech may be extremely hurtful and cruel, deceptive and misleading, defiling and contaminating, falsely accusatory, discouraging etc.

It could be that your attitude is extremely negative thereby releasing a negative energy and atmosphere wherever you go, or habits and behaviours that are offensive and despicable off-putting etc.

It could just be your nonverbal posture and the messages that flow out of that stance, which can be seen as offensive.

c. How is Your Leaking Issue Affecting Your Destiny?

"Blood" is commonly and generally known to represent life and vitality so when you "bleed" it means that you are being drained of life it and valuable energy which leaves you weak and disempowered and unable to effectively live your life and fulfil your Destiny.

So, where the bleeding entails losing valuable and necessary things out of your life it means that you are left inadequate with insufficient tools for fulfilling your Destiny (like provision, energy, passion, motivation resources, relationships, skills, and abilities etc.). It also means that the "bleeding" cripples you and immobilizes you from living a full life, participating in public and social life which leads to loneliness, isolation, and depression.

Where the "bleeding" is of the offensive kind, then it means that you become ostracized and rejected, side-lined and overlooked, whereby you lose favour and cannot access opportunities, resources, relationships, and places that you desperately need in order to fulfil your Destiny and Purpose. The bleeding becomes antisocial, so your public engagement is limited. Most tragic is that your bleeding attacks your ability to worship God.

There is a story of a woman in the bible in **Matthew 9:20-22**, which illustrates this point very well.

d. How Do You Stop This Leaking Issue?

You must proactively seek to know what choices, decisions and actions you need to make and take in order to lay hold of the "hem of your healing".

It takes desperate measures to deal with this situation, so it will require you to arise in radical faith in doing whatever you must to access your healing by saying enough is enough because you have suffered long enough and endured hard enough.

It will require you to make some serious Destiny decisions to show that the fulfilling your Destiny is more important than any embarrassment you may suffer in laying hold of your healing and that your Destiny is more important than dignity.

It will also entail a bold and courageous risk of breaking any established protocol in your way, overlooking any social cultures and traditions that may seek to oppress you as well as any poisonous peoples' opinions that may seek to intimidate you from accessing your healing and victory.

You must be willing to go low in humility to the point where you can lay hold of the hem of your healing, no matter how embarrassing, demeaning and humiliating. The Woman who is passionate enough in fulfilling her Destiny is one who is unapologetic about how low she may need to go to lay hold of her healing and Destiny.

Your victory over this leaking issue will in short entail your humility, passion, desperation and timing. Sitting at the feet of trusted mentors, coaches, counsellors, pastors and other such Destiny helpers will enable you to lay hold of valuable principles whether it be in your finances, social networks, spiritual walk etc.

Having a humble teachable spirit means acknowledging that there are people around us who carry the "healing we need and that we do not know it all".

Being desperate means we have suffered enough and lost too much and that no dignity will stand in our way because your dignity without a Destiny is hollow and meaningless.

Being passionate means putting your Destiny first above people, opinions and any culture or protocol.

Being within timing means, choosing your moment to execute your Destiny decisions in order to become whole again and clutch at your Destiny before it's too late.

4. WHAT IS YOUR THIRSTY THIRST?

(Are you quenching your void and emptiness from the right wells?)

"I drink because I'm thirsty." ~ Shane MacGowan

a. What Does Your Thirst Mean and Symbolize?

Thirst symbolizes a condition where you are empty and dry and unrefreshed having a deep longing and a yearning for something. It means you sense a lack of fulfilment in some area of your life.

To effectively deal with that thirst that affects your progress to your Destiny, it is important that you **firstly,** identify the particular thirst; **secondly** acknowledge your need to quench that thirst, and **thirdly** and most importantly seek the right well that will quench that thirst.

Your thirst may be;

- **Physical** where your **body** is sick and craving to be healed.
- **Emotional, social and relational** where you are lacking either peace, calmness, fulfilment, love, forgiveness, confidence, affirmation, self-esteem, healthy and meaningful relationships, and social interaction.

- **Mental and intellectual** where your mind is lacking stimulation, focus, or direction; where you are yearning for knowledge wisdom etc.
- **Financial** where you are yearning for financial acumen, financial abundance, and empowerment etc.
- **Spiritual** where you are yearning for a deeper relationship and walk with God, a deeper revelation of God's word and manifestation of God's promises over your life.

"A giant thirst is a great joy when quenched in time." ~ Edward Abbey

b. What is causing your thirst?

Your "**physical thirst**" is obviously coming from a lack of good health and hydration, so adequate and proper nutrition could be the solution.

Your "**emotional, social and relational thirst**" is either coming from having fallen into pits of emotional, relational and social abuse from which you have not yet healed. You need to seek healing and wellness before you can engage in other healthy meaningful relationships that are necessary for you to fulfil your Destiny.

Your "**mental and intellectual thirst**" is as a result of having fallen into the pits of mental and intellectual abuse from which you have not yet healed (because of wrong thoughts, negative mind-sets, injection of wrong information or indoctrination) and you are struggling to cleanse your mind back to purity.

Your "**financial thirst**" this is as a result of either neglecting to grow financially and expand by accessing the right financial principles and knowledge that you need. Or from having accessed the wrong financial principles and the wrong knowledge which is therefore not giving you the desired outcome.

Your "**spiritual thirst**" could either be as a result of your failure to pursue and chase God passionately enough or immerse yourself deeply enough in the word of God. You could be too busy focusing in the other areas of your life or as a result of positioning yourself in a wrong altar or place of worship where you are not receiving the right doctrines and teaching. It could be where you are being defiled and contaminated with what is fake.

c.   How is your thirst affecting your Destiny?

Your "thirst" whether physical, emotional, mental, financial, social, relational or spiritually, means that you are drying up. When something dries up enough, the next thing is to crack, break and die, meaning that continued thirst will lead you to such depths of frustration and despair that you literally give up and fail to fulfil your Purpose and Destiny.

Extreme and continued "thirst" in whatever area of your life, will lead to dehydration. Extreme dehydration is known to affect one's mind whereby you become delirious and delusional and become unable to function effectively thereby prejudicing your Destiny.

A "thirst" that you have not acknowledged will therefore cause you to become dry, infertile, unfruitful and unproductive. Worse still, failure to understand what kind of "thirst" you are suffering from or to understand which area of your life is "thirsty" may lead you to quench the wrong area in your life. Failure to understand what you require in order to quench a thirst in you will lead you to drink from the wrong well in an attempt to quench that "thirst."

For example, your real "thirst" maybe some meaningful healthy relationship with a father figure in order to quench and heal from a father wound but instead you may erroneously think that your "thirst" is for any man who will offer you comfort and physical intimacy which will put you in a worse state than you were before.

Or where you think that your "thirst" is for mountains of wealth and you rush into overnight get rich quick schemes, instead of quenching the real "thirst" which was for solid, progressive, understanding of sound well tested principles on wealth creation that will usher you into legitimate and long-lasting wealth with a Purpose.

d. How do you quench your thirst?

Your thirst will be quenched when you finally drink from the right well and then every other thirst in your life will be quenched.

You will need to acknowledge that you have a thirst and ascertain in which area of your life. Quenching your "thirst" will require you to locate the right well for each specific type of "thirst" in your life.

In your journey to Destiny, you will come across several and different types of wells some which will be pure and fresh and some which will be stale and contaminated, or poisoned or evil and it will be your responsibility to discern which well is which.

For example, there will be Wells of wisdom, and Wells of folly, Wells of honour and Wells of shame, Wells of friendship and Wells of loneliness, Wells of wealth and Wells of poverty, Wells of healing and Wells of pain, Wells of success, and Wells of failure etc.

There will be some Wells of strife which you will have to contend for, because there will be wells that you need to drink from but your enemies will seek to restrict and hinder you, by blocking and clogging those wells. So, you must fight and contend for those wells especially if they contain what you need for your Purpose and Destiny.

You will need to locate certain wells that were dug up for you by your fathers and from which your fathers drunk and after locating them you need to re-dig them, where they are clogged and drink from them because they are wells of your inheritance.

Some wells you will encounter will be dry wells and therefore useless to you and you must learn to walk away from dry wells. You will need to also learn how to dig your own wells and protect them from your enemies so that you may leave a good legacy of wells to your seed and the next generation.

You will also encounter wells of social interactions which will lead to marriage because it is when you are at the right well that you will be located. For example, several women in the bible became betrothed for marriage while at a well like, Rebecca.

It is at the "well of servanthood" that you will fulfil your service by being able to draw and quench others. It is at the right well that you will have the boldness to ask all the questions you need to ask and to receive all the wisdom and impartation that you need to receive. If you are willing to listen and have a teachable spirit and you are able to recognize and accept the truth graciously.

It is at the "bad girls' well" that you will be provoked and become vulnerable to share your story as to how you've been drinking from the "well of poor choices". It is at this well that you will receive compassion and deliverance and a revelation that your past and current mess, dysfunctional life style and confusion should not define you nor hinder your future and Destiny. It is at this well that you will be honest and you will experience a paradigm shift and see a different reality that will lead you to change or experience a dramatic transformation that will propel you to your Destiny.

It is also at the right well that you will get a revelation of how to quench your real "thirst" so that you may abandon every other useless well you have sought to quench your "thirst" from in vain. It is also at the right well that you will get valuable lessons that will empower you for Destiny.

Drawing from right Wells requires some deliberate decision and action and it is a personal responsibility which speaks to your Destiny choices.

John 4:13-14 – *"Jesus answered and said to her, "Whoever drinks of this water will thirst again, but whoever drinks of the water that I shall give him will never thirst. But the water that I shall give him will become in him a fountain of water springing up into everlasting life."*

At each Well, you encounter in your journey to Destiny, you must pause and ponder as to what lessons to draw from each well that will empower, wisen and transform you.

5. WHAT IS YOUR SQUINTY SIGHT?

(Are you allowing your outward appearance to undermine the fruitfulness within you?)

"He is short-sighted who looks only on the path he treads and the walls in which he leans." ~ Khalil Gibran

a. What does your squinty sight symbolize?

"Squinty eyes" symbolize a skewed perspective, a slanted way of seeing things. Squinty eyes distort the facial features thereby taking away the physical beauty of the face.

A squinty Vision also implies that you are not seeing things, people and situations properly because your "squintness". Your head seems to be facing in one direction yet your eyes are looking in a different direction. This means that your mind set, intentions and attitude are in total contradiction and not aligned so your view and perception is distorted and defective.

In the physical squintiness is where the eyes are looking in all different directions at the same time and it could symbolize that Woman is conflicted and double minded, instead of being single minded and focused and the result is that the vision will be blurred and distorted.

b. What is causing your squinty sight?

When you've lived long enough in the shadow of other people who are considered more beautiful than you, smarter than you, more talented, skilled and gifted than you, then over time you become accustomed to remain insignificant in the background in the "self-pity zone."

Subconsciously you learn to accept second place and second best and to clutch and hunger for every little attention that comes your way because deep down you don't feel entitled and deserving of any attention.

The continued chronic discrimination against you keeps you in a desperate place of pain and despair without any expectations that anything good can come your way. When you are side-lined long enough and your needs are never considered, you spend most of your life seeking love and approval, desperate for attention and affirmation, from anyone who can give it to you (irrespective of their motives for doing so). This puts you in a dangerously vulnerable position.

So, while your "squintiness" is initially inflicted by others, yet over time if you are not careful to resist and correct it, that squintiness will be reinforced by you and you will start to embrace it own it and normalize it.

Mat. 6:23 – *"But if your eye is bad, your whole body will be full of darkness. If therefore the light that is in you is darkness, how great is that darkness!"*

c. How is Your Squinty Sight Affecting Your Destiny?

Your "Squintiness" makes you so blinded because of the rejection and desperation to be loved that you end up compromising your Destiny. Your focus is in the wrong direction and on the wrong people so you become prone to making poor choices that are warped and based on your desperate need for people's approval.

Your "squintiness" makes you so insecure in who you are that you allow others to define you negatively which totally distorts your identity. When you fall into an identity crisis it becomes virtually impossible for you to make any right choices or to even be able to discover and embark on your Purpose and Destiny (because your ability to discover and fulfil you Purpose is fundamentally based on your ability to correctly define yourself and be secure in who you are).

"Squintiness" fills your head with a negative view of self, whereby you erroneously begin to define yourself by the wrong things (like material substance, success, children, social status etc.) instead of defining yourself by what pertains to your Purpose and Destiny.

"Squintiness" also makes you so distorted that you fail to enjoy the precious and beautiful things right in front of you because you are so busy chasing after worthless illusions that are out of your reach and that are not necessary for fulfilling your Purpose and Destiny. Furthermore, your squintiness hinders you from seeking your difference and your uniqueness that makes you special valid, valuable and relevant.

Sadly, the effects of "Squintiness" will often cause you to become a pawn in the deceptive schemes of others in fulfilling their wicked devices. Do not allow yourself to become an "AOB" in other people's agenda, instead be the "main item" in the "agenda" of your Purpose and Destiny.

d. How to Correct Your "Squintiness"?

Your squinty sight will be corrected when you birth a Judah and your praise shifts to God not man. **(Gen.29:35),** and you rest from birthing vanity.

You must come to a place when you stop chasing and seeking after things and relationships that are not necessary for your Destiny and shift your focus to pursuing and laying hold of those things and relationships that do matter and add value to your Destiny.

You must shift your mind set and attitude into believing that you are fearfully and wonderfully made and that your beauty is in the eyes of your creator. Any flaws that your Creator may have chosen to allow through in the mix, are intended to make you unique and God will still use everything within you to accomplish His Purpose for you.

Your physical and outward appearance whether it is considered attractive or not by others, should never be your setback and you must not allow it to affect your Destiny and you should look at other valuable aspects within you that are more important and more relevant for your Destiny than outward appearance.

6. WHAT IS YOUR BARRENNESS?

(Are you focusing on what breaks your barrenness or on what mocks your barrenness?)

"He remembers the barren." ~ Katie Schuermann

a. What does Barrenness Mean or Symbolize?

In your journey to Destiny, you will encounter many and different forms of "barrenness" whether physically, emotionally, socially, financially, relationally or spiritually which symbolizes a dryness, a lack, a fruitlessness, or an emptiness.

"Barrenness" implies that you are not producing or progressing as much as you would want to. It also implies that you are somehow stagnant and stuck in that particular area of your life because you are not seeing the result or outcome you desire and you are feeling that expectations are somewhat cut short.

"Beware of barrenness in a busy life." **By Socrates**

b. What is causing your "Barrenness"?

In the physical, barrenness is usually as a result of some infirmity or defect in the body thereby hindering successful conception whereby one is unable to receive and carry the seed and bring forth fruit.

Likewise, and symbolically, there could be areas in one's life (like business, career, relationships, spiritual walk, etc.) where you are unable to bear fruit as a result of several factors;

- **A hard and rocky womb** – where there is a hardness of heart caused by toxic emotions like anger, bitterness, offence, unforgiveness, past pain and failure. So, the seed once deposited is choked and unable to take root and bring forth a harvest. This requires a healing and casting out of these negative emotions so as to soften the environment and break the barrenness.

- **A dry womb** – where it is not sufficiently watered because you have not been drinking from the right wells. Instead, you have been drinking from dry wells. You need to start drinking from the wells of fruitfulness and abandon every well of fruitlessness for the seed to take root and bring forth fruit.

- **A defiled womb** – where you have been drinking from contaminated wells of a wrong mind-set, negativity, poverty mentality, low self-esteem, lack of self-confidence etc. Instead, you should be drinking from the pure fresh wells of an abundance mentality and a true identity for the seed to take root and bring forth fruit.

- **A hostile womb** – where as a result of external forces and attacks from the enemies of your Destiny like mockery, rejection, abandonment, that create a hostile atmosphere for the seed. You should engage with your Destiny helpers in order to defeat these attacks and erase this hostile environment for the seed to take root and bring forth fruit.

- **A confused womb** –where a lack of revelation as to what you want or need to conceive. This means that lack of understanding and failure to discover your Purpose and Destiny hinders you from conceiving. For the seed to take root and bring forth fruit, you need to get clarity on the who you were born to be and the what you were created to do etc.

- **A conflicted womb** – where there is such internal conflict and turmoil raging storms within you and there is no sufficient peace and calmness to enable the seed to take root and bring forth fruit. You need to come to a place of self-reflection, self-analysis so that you understand where you are coming from, where you are at and where you are going so that you can make the right choices and decisions to enable you conceive.

- **A passionless womb** – whereby there is no sufficient hunger, yearning or motivation to allow the seed to take root and bring forth fruit.

c. How Your is "Barrenness" Affecting Your Destiny?

Your "Barrenness" whether it be emotional or relational; financial or spiritual causes you to be rejected and be an outcast thereby denying you the opportunity to grow and develop in healthy relationships and environments.

Your "Barrenness" causes you to be mocked and stigmatized as one who is a curse thereby pushing you into isolation and ostracization.

Your "Barrenness" causes you to be rejected by even the closest around you who were expecting you to bring forth fruit for their benefit as well.

d. How to break your "Barrenness"

Psalms 113:9 – *"He grants the barren Woman a home, like a joyful mother of children. Praise the LORD!"*

Your bareness will break when you adopt a **"Hannah Hunger"** (1 Samuel 1).

i. Your "barrenness" will break because of your desperate passion for it to break and because of your deep travail.

ii. Your "**barrenness**" will break at your place of worship where you are at your most vulnerable, authentic and real and where the opinion of others no longer affect you. When you have no apology to make, when they see you indignified in desperation and yearning.

iii. Your "**Barrenness**" will break when you adamantly refuse to settle for less than that which you know you were created for (despite the persuasions of those who would want you to settle for the mediocre).

iv. Your "**Barrenness**" will break when you become wise enough to know that focusing and reacting to your mockers is a waste of valuable energy and time and that your total focus must be on those things and relationships that have the power to break your "**barrenness**".

v. Finally, your "**Barrenness**" will break when you make a vow that when you do bear fruit, you will dedicate that fruit to impact and transform the lives of so many other than yourself.

Isaiah 54:1 – *"Sing, O barren, you who have not borne! Break forth into singing, and cry aloud, you who have not labored with child! For more are the children of the desolate than the children of the married Woman," says the LORD."*

7. WHO SHORT-CHANGED YOU?

(Are you willing to leave your isolation and come to the palace at the king's table?)

"God is going to put you on somebody's mind who is in a position to restore what you lost." ~ Bishop T.D Jakes

a. What Does Your Short-Change Symbolize?

Often you may feel you were short-changed in a situation whereby, what you put into something or someone was not fairly rewarded. It basically means to get less than the correct amount of change or to be deprived of or be given less than what is due to you, but you walk away puzzled, yet sure you have been short-changed.

Being short-changed leaves you feeling cheated, fleeced, ripped off, exploited, taken advantage of etc. It may symbolize an implied and silent promise or a covenant that was silently broken where you were left or discarded, or dropped by those who you trusted and least expected to short-change you.

Your short changers are usually people in your life. It is where there is often a thin line between what you are entitled to and what must be earned, especially where there are also close emotional ties, honour and respect like your parents, employers, bosses, leaders etc.

b. What Causes You to Be Short-Changed?

Being short-changed arises from several different types or situations where you either sacrificially deliver services, give or invest resources, give your time, energy, commitment and loyalty in a situation, with the expectation that there will be payback time, only to later on come empty handed and unrewarded or even where rewarded you felt it was inadequate and disproportional to your input.

You may have been short-changed in a relationship, whether it was within the family, a friendship, a marriage or even a courtship. It is where you were so emotionally invested to the point of being sacrificial in giving up your own time, interests, goals, dreams and Visions. You faithfully gave yourself totally to that situation or maybe it was a business and professional scenario, where you invested skills, resources, ideas, concepts, knowledge and wisdom etc. or voluntary services you offered in serving someone or an institution etc.

Suffice to say that in all these situations, you had reasonable expectations of some kind of return, whether in the form of marriage, inheritance, promotion, monetary gains, favours, commendation etc. (whether it was expressly stated or not) and in your view the implication was clear and mutual.

Perhaps what makes your pain more acute is the trust you had and the goodwill with which you operated. Worse still is the fact that those who should have rewarded, compensated or at least remembered you, are persons with whom you cannot contend with by virtue of their status position and your respect for them. It could be that your expectation could have been sincerely misguided, plus no law has been broken after all.

c. How Does This Short-changing Affect Your Destiny?

This kind of pain point more or less paralyses you because you can't really talk or murmur about it without embarrassing yourself and looking foolish for having put yourself in such a position.

It silences you because, you have no "broken law" or "covenant" to stand on and your expectations could easily be termed as misguided and presumptuous. In addition, the respect and standing with, which your short changer is held by those around you, leaves you disadvantaged and without credibility.

The effect on you is disillusionment and regret, which makes you hardened and bitter, hindering you from moving on to fulfilling your Purpose because you develop serious trust issues in any relationship you encounter or opportunity that presents itself in the future.

In addition, the feelings of possibly having been made a fool of is humiliating and embarrassing, which only sharpens the pain point, not to mention the actual losses and delays you calculate as incurred by being short-changed.

Perhaps the real subtle struggle comes from the fact that you must continue relating with that short changer (whether they be family members, a potential suitor, business partners, political leaders, professional colleagues, bosses or spiritual authorities) who you feel short-changed you. You are not at liberty to display any untoward emotions etc. and everyone behaves as if nothing wrong was ever done and its business as usual.

d. **Do You Know How to Heal After Being Short-changed?**

- **Firstly**, healing from this pain point and turning it into a power point is to acknowledge you were short-changed, clearly and squarely (as opposed to not being sure or being in denial yet hurting inside).

- **Secondly**, it is to examine the situation or relationship that gave rise to this short-change critically and check whether your expectations were off base and unrealistic and

- **Thirdly** share the facts with a trusted, mature, Destiny helper like a coach or mentor and get a clear understanding of your pain and what to do about it.

- **Fourthly** it may be feasible to politely "confront" the perceived short changer and pour your heart out respectfully, because sometimes letting someone know they hurt and disappointed us could be the healing (even where no actual restitution is made).

- **Fifthly** and in the alternative, it may be that letting it go without any confrontation is more prudent, and you work on forgiving and forbearing in order to enable you move on and make more gain.

The valuable life lessons learnt from a short change situation could be the very healing you need, so that you will know better next time.

Ensure you never short-change anyone yourself, because you know how it feels and also choosing to maintain a positive attitude towards future opportunities to serve, collaborate and invest in others and to extend trust again is crucial.

You may get pleasantly surprised when one day those you thought had forgotten your contributions into their lives, send for you, and reward you at a time you least expected.

Just always remember that any pain point or subtle struggle you encounter and experience in your journey to destroy will push you to your Destiny depending on how you choose to respond to it, and chances are that God himself may have allowed that short-changing to teach you certain valuable lessons for your future. So, the sooner you let it go and move on, the sooner you will learn and apply those lessons.

"Sometimes pain can teach us lessons that we didn't think we needed to know." ~ Unknown

Destiny Questions to Ponder On

1. *How have you overcome your **Salty pillar**?*

2. *What issue in particular do you believe causes your own **Bendedness**?*

3. *Is your **Leaky issue** that of positive valuable things or that of negative offensive things?*

4. *What emptiness are you experiencing in your life, have you located the right **Wells** to quench your **Thirst**?*

5. *What finally corrected your **squinty sight**?*

6. *How do you respond to your mockers during your **Barrenness**?*

7. *How close to you was the person who **short-changed** you?*

This Page Was Intentionally Left Blank

Chapter 5

THE PITSTOPS OF A DESTINY RACER

Refueling At Defining Moments In Your Journey

Chapter Preview

1. **The Wrestling to your Blessing**

    (*Battling for your true identity and name*)

2. **The Altar of idols**

    (*Burying your past in order to enter your future*)

3. **The Valley of Vanity**

    (*Regrowing your hair and Regaining your authority.*)

4. **The Labour of Deceit**

    (*Escaping from your place of exploitation*)

5. **The Den of Despair**

    (*Encouraging yourself, pursuing and recovering all.*)

6. **The Crossroad To Your Destiny**

    (*Owning your Damascus moment*)

7. **The River of Circumcision**

    (*A painful crossing to your place of power.*)

OPENING REMARKS

In your journey to Destiny, you will pass many significant places (whether they be caves, pits, valleys, peaks, rivers, roads, dens, wildernesses etc.) that will be grounds for learning valuable lessons to propel you to each new beginning and new level towards your Destiny.

During the Renowned Worldwide Formula One races, the driver has to make regular pit stops for Purposes of refuelling and having a wheel change etc. which empowers his ability to race even faster. Despite the seconds that he may lose at the pit stop, the speed at which he will then move is doubled making the seconds at the pit stop worthwhile.

Likewise, and symbolically the Purpose of "pit stops" in your journey to Destiny is to give you an opportunity to confront an issue or issues in your life that are threatening to slow you down and derail you and to that extent these are crucial learning curves and growth spots that actually speed up and accelerate your journey.

It is important to understand these growth spots in terms of what they symbolize and mean. What causes you to come to such a growth spot, what impact does each growth spot have on you and your Destiny, what response, actions, choices and decisions will you need to make to move on from that growth spot empowered.

Most importantly what lessons will you have learnt from that growth spot which you can hopefully use in handling other growth spots that you will inevitably come to, in the remaining portion of your journey to Destiny.

Each of these growth spots will grow a different aspect in your life, and fortify you further for the journey.

To successfully grow from a pitstop, you will need to accept and embrace change and transformation.

1. THE WRESTLING TO YOUR BLESSING

(Battling For Your Name And Identity)

a. What does the wrestling wilderness symbolize?

Your wrestling wildernesses will force you into the ring to fight the battle within you, in order to find your real self. Your striving and struggling will leave you with a "**defining limb**" to forever remind who you were born to be and you will leave that wilderness with a "**new name**" and having found your real self-identity and Purpose.

Every time you display and manifest "a who" you were not born to be, there will be a struggle and striving within you, an agony and a torment that will not be silenced until you have engaged an intense wrestling and found the real you.

So, your wrestling wilderness will symbolize a place where you will confront an internal conflict in your identity. It symbolizes a very personal and intimate struggle and inner wrestling so that your real identity may come out and you may let go of everything else you have allowed to define you that should not have defined you.

This growth spot will therefore confront your identity disorder and grow you into the who you were born to be.

Your wrestling wilderness is a midnight hour when all your past pain, frustrations, fears, doubts, anxieties, insecurities and everything else that has sought to erode and distort your identity will gush out and you cannot avoid them. Each issue is demanding that you address it before you can move forward. It is a place of defining choices and decisions where you cannot rely on anybody else but your maker. So, it is a very personal experience, where you must separate yourself from everyone else, in order to find yourself without other people's projections.

b. **What causes your wrestling wilderness?**

By the time you find yourself at a wrestling wilderness, it is because you have taken on a false identity and allowed yourself to be defined in a certain way, because of your dysfunctional behaviours and habits (whether it be dishonesty, manipulation, leaning on your own limited understanding and human wisdom).

You find yourself at the wrestling wilderness because you have long convinced yourself that trickery, cunningness and shortcuts are the means by which you will fulfil your Destiny, probably because you are trying to be smarter than your creator.

A wrestling wilderness is a place you must come to after you have realized that your self-devised methods and short cuts will not get you to your Destiny because there is a process, set steps and principles for fulfilling your Purpose and Destiny, which you must adhere to.

You will eventually come to this wrestling wilderness place after you have escaped from your self-inflicted wilderness (where you were exploited, manipulated, oppressed and kept in bondage until you said enough is enough and you escaped). Maybe it is an abusive marriage, a toxic place of work, a bad business partnership or a dictatorial political regime etc. that is holding you back from your Purpose and Destiny.

A wrestling wilderness is where you have reached your end and you have suffered enough and exhausted all your self-defeating devices which have not worked. You finally become desperate and you want to seek and adopt the right ways to your Destiny. Your agony and restlessness is so intense, you cannot take another step without a radical transformation that will set you free from your torment and the raging battle within you.

You will find yourself at a wrestling wilderness because you had de-positioned yourself from your true place of assignment and Purpose, due to your own deceptive dealings, bad choices, and actions.

c.   What are the effects of a wrestling wilderness on your Destiny?

Your wrestling wilderness has the effect of subduing you and humbling you into an acceptance of the right way to your Destiny and a surrendering and a letting go of your stubborn and carnal ways.

Your wrestling wilderness will usher you into a new dawn and a new beginning. As you walk away from your wrestling wilderness, you will have a "limp" that will forever remind you and others that you have come out of a dark wrestling season that has radically transformed you, defined your true identity and given you a new name that has empowered you towards fulfilling your Purpose and Destiny.

Your wrestling wilderness strips you of every wrong identity you had allowed yourself to walk in. it heals every dysfunctional behaviour, mind-set, unhealthy emotions and negative stigma. It matures you into understanding that a new name comes with new responsibilities and that you have wrestled for your new name and true identity in order to lay hold of your true Purpose blessings and Destiny.

A wrestling wilderness is the place where you become fully persuaded that you can only thrive and fulfil your Destiny at your appointed and ordained place of Purpose and blessing.

You must return to your place of Purpose and blessing irrespective of the fear you have of facing the people you angered and left there.

d. How do you thrive at your place of wrestling?

At your wrestling place you must wrestle with every issue that you need to confront in your life. You must wrestle until you have had a breakthrough on every issue that has conflicted you and caused such turmoil within you, (whether it be deep regret for bad choices, lost opportunities and missed miles, or the pain of mistreatment and exploitation, or even the fear and dread of encountering people you hurt and wronged).

At your wrestling place you must Purpose that the darkness and pain will not stop you from wrestling, because for your dawn and light to come, there must be a darkness and pain to endure.

In other words, at your wrestling place, you must put your desire for your light and dawn higher than your fear for the darkness and pain. Only then will you successfully leave that wrestling place and move on. It's a place for defining Destiny decisions and choices.

At your wrestling wilderness, you are encountering your identity and your Destiny. You must therefore engage through intense faith and prayer and you must rely on the strength of the promises over your life. You must not stop wrestling until you have laid hold of your true identity, your new name and your new dawn.

The '**limp**' from your wrestling place symbolizes an identity deeper than a name, because it comes from a touch and the finger prints of your Owner and Maker – the God of your wrestling place and the God of your Destiny.

2. THE ALTAR OF IDOLS

(Burying Your Past in Order to Enter Your Future)

a. What does the altar of idols symbolize?

At the **"altar of idols"** you will have to bury every false worship, wrong focus, strange burden and carnal obsessions that you acquired in your place of exile, in order to return to your place of Purpose and claim your inheritance, towards your Destiny.

This is where you will call into question, the legitimacy or validity of all the false things, carnal obsessions and practices that you have allowed yourself to embrace that contradict your Purpose and Destiny.

The **"altar"** means and symbolizes a place where you must let go and bury every idol in your life that is hindering you from your Destiny and that is seeking to kill you. Your altar of idols is a place where you must make a Destiny decision and choice whether you want to leave your ugly place of exploitation and return to your place of blessings and Destiny.

Whenever you choose to plan your exit from your place of exploitation and struggle and to return to your place of Purpose and blessings, you will encounter certain elements (whether internal or external) seeking to entangle and hinder you on the eve of your exit.

The altar of idols is literally one day's journey away from your place of Purpose and blessings, but no matter how near it is you cannot access it until you have buried all your idols, carnal obsessions and strange burdens. It is the place where you must disconnect yourself physically, mentally, socially, spiritually and emotionally from anything that has consumed and obsessed you and which has threatened the fulfilment of your Destiny.

Whether it be unhealthy relationships, obsessions with wealth and material substance, a bloated ego and social status, prideful positions of power and influence, stale success and outdated accomplishments etc.

The returning must be with pure motives and unencumbered so that your restoration to your true Purpose and place is on a right and strong foundation.

b. **What causes you to come to the altar of idols?**

Sometimes we may knowingly or unknowingly begin to practice idolatry by placing our trust and hope and worship on the wrong things and we shift our focus to dead things.

When we have suffered chronic disappointments and failures and we have gone through one wilderness after another and our pain blinds us from the right path because our faith is shaken and we begin to doubt what we once believed.

Often you will find yourself at this place of idolatry because you are escaping from another place of hardship, lack, suffering and despair. You unknowingly carry with you these strange things through the relationships you have allowed in your life and the idolatrous practices you have picked up from the wrong places you took yourself.

These idolatrous things and practices threaten to blind your Vision, attach themselves to your heart and soul and hold you back from your Destiny because they are things that you have a strong and deep emotional and mental attachment to, and you must burn and bury them in order to move on.

c. How Does the Altar of Idolatry Affect Your Destiny?

This place has a good impact for your Destiny because it shows a positive and progressive action on your part to retrace your steps back to your place of assignment and Purpose.

At this place you get a revelation about what is holding you back and killing your Destiny and hence your radical Destiny decision to bury your past and build your future, so as to enable you cross over and fulfil your Destiny.

It is the place where after burying your idols, your eyes are opened and you finally arise and take up your rightful authority to re-discover your Purpose. It is the place where you rename everything in your life that others had sort to misname, whether it be your children, business, career, your Purpose and Destiny.

d. How to grow away from the altar of Idolatry

At this growth spot, you must regain your rightful authority as the master of your Destiny, and you put your Destiny first before your emotional attachments and obsessions, and offload every baggage that has held you back from your place of Purpose and Destiny.

The action of burning and burying all your idols is the key that opens the gates to your return and restoration to your Purpose and place and blessings. It is the action that resurrects and reactivates the passion and gifts within you for your Purpose.

3. THE VALLEY OF VANITY

(Regrowing Your Hair And Regaining Your Power)

a. What a Valley of Vanity Symbolizes?

At your **"valley of vanity"**, once you have realized the consequences of your poor and bad choices, you will arise with a provoked fury and regained strength and manifest who you were born to be, and you will fulfil the Purpose you were called to fulfil, even if you have to die doing so.

This valley of vanity symbolizes a place which is down and below (rather than above and high) because it is a valley, meaning you have downgraded yourself to a lower level physically, emotionally, morally, financially, socially and spiritually etc., thereby weakening your influence, value and relevance.

This valley is **"enemy territory"** to you because it is where everything fights your Destiny, like idolatry, evil soul ties, unhealthy obsessions, canal desires and lusts, wrong connections, wrong environments and atmospheres, wrong habits and behaviours, inappropriate dressing or outward adornment, profane speech, suspect and questionable business deals, shaky doctrines and new beliefs not tested etc. It symbolizes a place where you may have been lured to, by stepping out of the path of your Destiny to seek carnal pleasure, it is the domain of your enemies so you should not even be there in the first place.

So, in other words it is a place of self-inflicted destruction, because you begin to partake and condone the very evils of the enemy you were called to destroy.

It is a place where you lose your strength and influence, because you have already de-positioned yourself from your place of Purpose.

No matter how gifted and strong we may be as women of Destiny, there are still some weaknesses within us, which will be kept in check as long as we remain in our right Purpose and right place.

The minute we disobediently deposition ourselves from that right Purpose and place, those weaknesses begin to manifest and thrive and our strengths begin to diminish. This is because of our confidence in self, pride, and poor moral judgments. These weaknesses within us make us vulnerable to our Destiny killers.

b. What leads you to the valley of vanity?

One of the reasons that you may find yourself in the valley of vanity is because you do not have a sufficient enough revelation of the who you were born to be (the person) and the what you were created to do (the Purpose) and the where you were called to impact and influence (the place).

Perhaps it could be that you have no revelation as to why you have been gifted and anointed. As long as you do not understand the Purpose of the gifts, power and strength you have, then chances are, you will always misuse them or misdirect them to the wrong Purpose, place and people.

By the time we get to the valley of vanity it is because we have deviated from our Purpose and Destiny and we have allowed ourselves to lose focus and direction. We may have put our own fleshly desires and indulgences before our Destiny. It could be because we have become so over-confident in our strength, power, gifting that we assume that we can enter into enemy territory and still survive because we have done it so many times before and gotten away with it.

Your "Enemy territory" differs from another person's enemy territory so you must discern and keep away from what represents "enemy territory" to you. Your "enemy territory" could be for example money, illicit substances, illicit relationships etc. that feed your weaknesses. The solution is to keep away from such temptations that weaken you.

c.   How does the valley of vanity affect your Destiny?

At this valley your recklessness and disobedience are likely to cause you to lose or jeopardize your strength, power and gifting which prejudices your ability to fulfil Destiny, and your actions causes your enemies to mock you, belittle you and humiliate you and enslave you.

At this valley you lose clear Vision for your Destiny and you have to rely on your enemies to see where you're going, which is not only laughable but dangerous. In the process you lose your honour, respect, dignity, your self-identity is eroded. Without a clear and secure identity, you cannot really secure your Purpose and Destiny.

Remember that your Purpose includes a people who you were called to impact positively and by sliding into this valley of vanity and endangering yourself and prejudicing your own Destiny, you also prejudice the people you were created and born to protect, defend and benefit by allowing yourself to be bound by the enemy making you ineffective for your people.

By being at this valley in the captivity of your enemies, you have already de-positioned yourself from the place of assignment and Purpose which means that you have de-positioned yourself from your place of power, protection and blessings where you thrive because you cannot thrive anywhere else outside of your place of Purpose and assignment.

d. How to survive and thrive at the valley of vanity

Fortunately, being a child of Destiny, (though with episodes of disobedience) means that there's a certain grace that is often extended to you by God, from time to time because as stated elsewhere, your Destiny will always fight for you. It will even follow you to the valley of vanity in order to hopefully salvage you.

So once you wake up and come to a place of sincere regret and remorse. You get a revelation as to "the who" you were born to be and "the what" you were created to do. That revelation will restore your power and strength and enable you to arise once again and destroy the what you were created to destroy, even if it means sacrificing yourself in the process.

Suffice to say that, you do end up fulfilling your Destiny, in an ironic sort of way (because your Purpose was to destroy those enemies and protect your people) and perhaps that in itself is comfort enough. Hopefully you will learn;

...**firstly,** that your Destiny will fight for you because it yearns to be fulfilled,

...**secondly**, you also learn the power of second chances and that the consequences of your wrong choices may sometimes mean fulfilling your Destiny at a very high cost.

...**thirdly,** that even if you lose your hair (which symbolizes your strength, power and authority), it will grow back again, when you remember who you were born to be and what you were created to do.

4. THE LABOUR OF DECEIT

(Escaping From Your Place Of Exploitation)

a. What Does this Labour of Deceit Symbolize?

At the **"labour of deceit",** your own dysfunctional behaviour and bad choices will confront you until you escape that place and retrace your steps back to your place of Purpose and blessings.

A labour of deceit addresses and confronts the unmoulded aspects of our character.

A labour of deceit is a growth spot in your journey to Destiny that symbolizes a place where you have taken refuge because you are running away from your own dysfunctional deceptive behaviour and past.

It turns out to be a place where you encounter people who are more deceptive and dysfunctional than you, and you are exploited and you get a taste of your own medicine. The reason you are at this place in the first place is because maybe you had exploited other people's weaknesses, whether as an employer, boss, leader etc. Or you had taken shortcuts and employed deceptive means to get your own way and will in whatever circumstances.

A labour of deceit, symbolizes a place of oppression and hardship and sorrow where your labour is not rewarded. It is a place of limitation and suffocation because you are not progressing as you should towards your real Destiny.

A labour of deceit is a place where you are more or less enslaved, reluctantly serving the interests of another and where you are constantly short-changed and suffer gross injustices.

It is a place where the rewards of your service and labour are grossly disproportionate, but you have no say or power to change that. You have lost your power and influence by moving away from your place of Purpose, into a self- inflicted exile which is a place of disadvantage and weakness. You have run away from your place because of the consequences of your wrong behaviour whether it was within your family, workplace, society, church, community etc.

A labour of deceit is not your permanent destination, so it also represents a place of hiding and making where your character is moulded before you can return to your Purpose and place of blessing. So, in a way, it is also a place of protection, preservation and a place to learn critical Destiny lessons that will equip and empower you going forward.

It is a crucial pit stop for your self-growth and development to empower you to fulfil your Purpose and Destiny.

b. What leads you to this labour of deceit?

More importantly, labour of deceit becomes a place where we have a "taste of our own medicine". We may reap all the negative things we have sown in the lives of others until we realize the consequences of our actions, and come out transformed for the better.

This labour of deceit is where your ability and willingness to submit to authority and leadership and surrender to servant hood is tested even where the leader and authority is harsh, oppressive and unjust. Yet you must remain submitted until that season ends and you have learnt the lessons of that growth spot like the grace to endure hardship and suffering, without resisting and rebelling.

This labour of deceit is the place where you may become emotionally attached and obsessed to things and relationships that later threaten your ability to return to your right Purpose and place unless you bury and burn those attachments and obsessions.

c. How does this sheepfold of deceit affect your Destiny?

At this labour of deceit, you learn crucial and valuable skills, wise strategies and how to outmanoeuvre your exploiters. You also learn the difference between outright deception and the smart use of your skills and gifts to get ahead and not only survive this season but also thrive.

Your season in this labour of deceit must come to an end eventually, and it will only come to an end when you become restless and uncomfortable, because you have learnt the lessons you needed to learn and exhausted your capacity there and you need to move on because you have outgrown the place.

Your labour of deceit will come to an end the day you realize that it was not your destination and that as long as you remain in there you are not making any meaningful progress to your Destiny.

Your labour of deceit season will also come to an end when your yearning for your Purpose and your place of blessing becomes so strong that you cannot spend one more night here. So, you must get up and break the yoke of bondage leave, irrespective of the attempts to keep you there.

d. How to survive and thrive at your labour of deceit

Your labour of deceit season will come to an end when your memory awakens and you remember who you were born to be and what you were created to do and where you were born to do it. It is at that point you will arise and make a radical Destiny decision and choice to embark on understanding your person, discovering your Purpose, locating your place of Purpose, identifying your people of Destiny.

Leaving this labour of deceit means you have made a decision to face and overcome the fear of your past and that you must make peace with your past in order to lay hold of your future and return to your rightful place of Purpose.

Often it is our regretful past that stands between our labour of deceit and our future and Destiny. So, we must deal and overcome that past, and get it out of the way.

However, remember that the only valuable thing from your past are the lessons you have learnt from it and you must not allow your past to offer you any help other than those lessons lest you fall back into its bondage. Just make peace with it and then remain separated and distant as you forge on to your future and Destiny.

It is important to note that before facing and overcoming your past, you will have encountered your night of wrestling (where your real identity is revealed) and hence you will have the ability to overcome your past. This is because of your new found confidence at who you are. You can never overcome your past unless you have come to a place of being secure in your true identity.

5. THE DEN OF DESPAIR

(Encouraging Yourself, Pursuing and Recovering All)

a. What Does the Den of Despair Symbolize?

At the **"den of despair"** you must arise from your wallow and self-pity and become your own greatest encourager as you pursue, overtake and recover all that the enemy has taken from you.

A den of despair is a place you will often come to in your journey to Destiny after you have experienced great calamities and disasters like the loss of your loved ones, the robbery of your hard-earned wealth, the destruction of a Vision that you have laboured so hard for, the unjust denial of positions and blessings that you have sacrificed so much for or the breakdown of significant and valuable relationships that you have paid such a high price to maintain.

These disasters, calamities and tragedies were either self-inflicted by our reckless errors of judgment, poor and bad choices or they were externally inflicted by our Destiny killers and other outside forces. We may face such a deep discouragement, which will overwhelm us and threaten to take us out.

Despair is a very strong and crippling emotion which causes hopelessness, loss of confidence and enthusiasm, motivation and you feel extremely disheartened and demoralized and all you want to do is quit and give up.

So, your den of despair is a place you come to when you feel you have done your best and given your all but for some reason or other you don't see any fruit for your labour and efforts. Even more painful is that those you have sacrificed for, do not seem to appreciate you and your efforts. They make it worse by actually blaming you and criticizing you when things go wrong and instead of supporting you and encouraging you, they want to stone you.

The den of despair is a popular place especially for those who are in positions of leadership and influence or who have responsibility over others, (whether in your family, society, social groups, business, church, political, or corporate sector). The den of despair is a growth spot that you will inevitably come to and not only once but several times in your journey to Destiny. The painful revelation you get is that those you expect support from are the very ones that will abandon you first.

b. What Has Led You to This Den of Despair?

- **Accumulated stress** – You will often find yourself at the den of despair as a consequence of several factors which include accumulated stress. This is where you have worked so hard for so long and you have done your best to remain positive and strong despite all the challenges you have encountered and the hurdles you have had to jump over.

  Not only have you remained strong for yourself but you have remained strong for the many others that you have been carrying and for whom you are responsible. The nature of your Purpose and Calling requires you to be strong for others and to encourage them without showing your own discouragement and you reach a point where that accumulated stress is too much for you. You literally grind to a halt and fall into a pit of an imaginable despair, due to the acute pressure, tension and strain, physically, emotionally and mentally.

- **Battle fatigue** – The other factor why you find yourself at the den of despair is due to battle fatigue where you have fought so hard and for so long without sufficiently resting your physical body and mind and because you are human you reach a point of extreme tiredness as a result of the emotional, mental and physical exertion which can even lead to illness.

- **Post victory anti-climax**-Another factor that brings you to the den of despair is "post victory anti-climax" which normally occurs ironically after you have experienced a great victory, accomplishment or success. The toll of getting that victory success or accomplishment literally comes tumbling down in an anti-climax which makes you lose sight and fail to appreciate that victory accomplishment and success.

- **Melt down**- Yet another factor is a meltdown and burnout which is a disastrous collapse or breakdown caused by chronic frustration and anxiety and feelings of being emotionally overwhelmed by the intensity and volume of your responsibilities or tasks.

- **Chronic disappointments** -Perhaps one of the most common factors that leads us to the den of despair is chronic disappointments, failures, unmet expectations and feelings of being short-changed. You feel that your diligent sowing, faithful servanthood and commitment in fulfilling your Purpose is only being rewarded with dead ends which causes you great confusion and despair.

All these factors bring you to a breaking point and sometimes the thing that finally pushes you over the edge, the "straw that broke the camel's back" is normally such a small non-issue in comparison to the gigantic things that brought you here.

So those around you may often be shocked because they don't understand how such a small issue could have such a devastating effect on you (but little do they know that this 'straw' is just a catalyst for the accumulated stress, battle fatigue, frustrations and disappointments).

- **How does your den of despair affect your Destiny?**

Your arrival at the den of despair irrespective of what factor brought you there will obviously impact on your Destiny in one way or another. It is incumbent upon you to quickly make a decision that your experiences at the den of despair will not destroy you or cause undue delay in your journey.

This is because a den of despair can easily stagnate you and paralyze you to the point where you lose irredeemable time and opportunities, (if you allow yourself to wallow in self-pity and clothe yourself with a victim syndrome).

This den can also seriously erode your confidence whereby you question whether you were actually called and what your Calling is. Even if you still believe you were called and you know your Calling you may begin to doubt whether you have what it takes to fulfil that Calling. This will fling you into a fatal faith crisis which could take you years to recover from and thereby prejudice your Destiny.

You may also experience a lot of bitterness and resentment towards those who abandoned you and who had the audacity to blame you for their calamity which they seem to have forgotten was also your calamity.

Finally, another common effect that a den of despair may have on your Destiny is to mislead and misguide you to settle for a lesser Purpose and Destiny which in your view will not demand too much of you. This is because you fear that your expectations may be disappointed again and you therefore seek to lower those expectations as a way of safeguarding and cushioning yourself.

- **How to Survive and Thrive at Your Den of Despair**

As a Woman serious about her Destiny, you must make an irrevocable resolve that nothing (whether good or bad) will ever hinder you from ultimately fulfilling your Purpose and Destiny. This resolve will help you to manage every setback that you experience by having a very clear understanding that **firstly** setbacks will come and **secondly** that overcoming those setbacks is not a luxurious option at your disposal but a mandatory requirement.

So, this den of despair is just another setback that you must see as a growth point and learn as many lessons as you can from it, as you continue to fulfil your Calling and Destiny.

After you leave the den of despair your responsibility towards people that you were called to impact and transform must remain intact and herein lies the mark of a mature Seasoned leader and Destiny winner.

It is at the den of despair you will learn the power of self–motivation and self-encouragement and the mark of a true leader that will enable you to come out of this den empowered.

Beyond learning these lessons, you will build up enough resolve faith and courage to pursue, overtake and recover everything the enemy has sought to take away from you and to grow stronger from this growth point.

6. **THE CROSSROAD TO YOUR DESTINY**

(Owning Your Damascus Moment)

a. **What Does the Damascus Moment Symbolize?**

When you come to the road to your real Destiny you will

experience a 'Damascus moment' which is a radical paradigm shift that will set you on the right path towards the real Purpose you were created for.

You may have been very zealous and extremely committed in fulfilling a Purpose that turns out to be a wrong and misguided Purpose. It is equivalent to journeying on the wrong road which will not get you to your right destination. It is like running the wrong race or running the right race in the wrong lane. And no matter how diligently you do so and even if you win, it is of no consequence and relevance because you tragically ran the wrong race to the wrong destination and you fulfilled the wrong Purpose that was not ordained for you.

Many of us in our zeal to get going and climb the power of success and the podium of accomplishments, may fail to first discover the specific Purpose that we were created to fulfil. In our misguided zeal we end up embarking on whatever appeals to us or looks exciting, profitable and sometimes fame oriented. Some may seek to become leaders when they do not have a leadership call or preachers when they have not been called to the pulpit etc.

A "Damascus moment" also occurs when you may have discovered your correct Purpose and Calling but you are purporting to fulfil it in the wrong place or sphere so that for example while you have been called to the sphere and mountain of church you end up taking yourself to the mountain and sphere of politics and governance etc.

As long as you are not positioned in your ordained place of Purpose you cannot effectively fulfil that Purpose.

Other instances are where you are seeking to transform and impact the wrong target group say the youth whereas your real target group are the women.

But a moment will come when in the midst of your misguided zeal, you get a radical shift and transformation and you come to an understanding that you were headed in the wrong direction fulfilling the wrong Purpose in the wrong place with the wrong people. It is at this critical point that you must embrace and own your **"Damascus moment"** and your blindness will be broken and you begin to see clearly and get on to the right Purpose.

A Destiny Woman must humbly accept and embrace her **Damascus moment** and proceed to fulfil her real Destiny instead of resisting and dying on the wrong road to the wrong Destiny.

b. What Has Caused You to Be on the Wrong Road?

The reason most of us end up on the wrong road, race and Purpose is because we went to the wrong sources to discover our Purpose and Calling. People who have no revelation as to who you were called to be and what you were called to do will mislead you either knowingly or unknowingly.

Or sometimes our motivation for pursuing a particular Purpose and Calling is based on a desire to glorify self, selfish ambition, love of money and material substance, pride for fame and accolades.

At other times our motivation for pursuing a particular Purpose is based on bias and prejudice and our own misguided judgment of people whereby we develop a racial or tribal resentment and we make it our Mission to 'correct' and transform those people.

All these will lead you in the wrong direction into the wrong Purpose, place and people etc.

c. The Effects of Your Damascus Moment on Your Destiny

The effects of being in the wrong Purpose (race, road, place or people) will seriously delay your journey to Destiny and misuse your valuable time, energy, gifts, skills and resources which you should have been using for your right Purpose.

It will also deny you access to crucial and significant relationships who you would have encountered had you been in your right Purpose and in your right place.

The other effects of experiencing, owning and embracing a **"Damascus moment"** is that the truth will set you free and it will also empower you to now get in the right Purpose and place towards your Destiny. Keep in mind that while you were in the wrong Purpose, place and people, you were not thriving nor were you as effective as you could have been because you can only thrive and maximize your effectiveness when you are in the right place, Purpose and people.

Your gifts will manifest and operate most when you are in the right Purpose and place but they will lie dormant or at best operate at half measure when you are in the wrong place and Purpose.

d. How To Survive and Thrive at Your Damascus Moment

- **Firstly,** you will survive and go on to thrive from a Damascus moment by owning and embracing it as opposed to resisting it and

- **Secondly** you must go to the right source in order to ascertain your right Purpose, place and people and

- **Thirdly,** you must seek to redeem the lost time and wasted opportunities by diligently seeking to understand your right Purpose, dedicate and commit yourself to it, locate your place of Purpose and position yourself there logistically and strategically and identify your Destiny relationships and your people to enable you make maximum progress in your journey and

- **Fourthly**, you must also Purposefully and intentionally undergo a radical mind set change, whereby you die to self as regards to all that you had erroneously embraced and become emotionally entangled with, when you were in the wrong Purpose and place.

You must come to a place of totally surrendering to your Purpose and Destiny.

Surviving and thriving your **"Damascus moment"** will also require you to discern and realign the gifts within you towards your right Purpose and seek to sharpen and harness them for their rightful and maximum use.

Your testimony as to how you had a **Damascus moment** will form crucial lessons that you must share with others who are on the wrong road so that they can have their Damascus moment.

Closely related to a **Damascus moment** is a "burning bush experience" where like in a Damascus Moment, you come to a radical paradigm shift as to the who you were born to be and the what you were created to do, and as to the who you have been sent.

7. THE RIVER OF CIRCUMCISION

(A Painful Crossing to Your Place Of Power)

a. What does the river of circumcision mean and symbolize?

At the **"river of circumcision"** you will encounter the leader in you and the painful revelation that you and your people must cut off everything that threatens to drown you, as you cross over to your place of blessing.

Your river of circumcision is a place you will come to where you will need to cross over to your place of abundance and blessings from your place or lack but there will be conditions that you must fulfil so that you may qualify to cross over.

It is a place where you are moving to a new level of greater influence and impact, more resources, more effectiveness and fruitfulness towards your Destiny.

Circumcision symbolizes the cutting away of things in your life, in your Purpose and Calling that are unprofitable burdensome and negative which threaten to slow down your fulfilment of your Purpose and Destiny or cause an abortion of Purpose.

It is a painful process because it seeks to uproot and cut out things that have become deeply embedded in you over a long period of time and getting them out will require "cutting" deeply and sharply.

It also symbolizes your consecration cleansing and purifying from things that have sought to defile and contaminate you (mentally and emotionally, socially, spiritually etc.) by entrenching in you a wrong mind-set, negative and toxic emotions and desires that hinder you from progressing forward and upwards.

A consecration will often precede or come together with a circumcision. It entails a separating and dedicating of yourself to your Purpose and a washing and flushing out of every flesh carnality filth and toxic thing that hinders you from that Purpose.

Whatever sphere or place of Purpose you have been called to, (whether in the sphere of political leadership, sphere of business and economic empowerment, sphere of impartation of wisdom and knowledge through education, sphere of Christian ministry and church, sphere of media or sphere of arts and entertainment etc.), your river of circumcision will be a place where you are crossing over to become more and do more.

b. What brings you to the river of circumcision?

The reason you have come to this place is because you have become uncomfortable in the place where you are at. You have outgrown it and you are now ready for higher and greater things that will translate into greater influence and impact as you fulfil your Purpose.

For you to accomplish all these you must crossover from where you are whether physically, emotionally, mentally or otherwise to lay hold of the new level on the other side of your crossing. The other reason you find yourself at the river of circumcision is because you have qualified to cross over to greater responsibilities but you must be "matured" into them through the symbolic circumcision of cutting away any excesses within you.

c. What effects does the river of circumcision have on your Destiny?

Your painful crossing has the effect of accelerating your journey to Destiny, it has the effect of empowering and equipping you more to do more and to provoke others to follow suit.

The crossing empowers us for the next battle and guarantees us victory over our enemy. Our circumcision and crossing over gives us the grace and courage to possess our inheritance. Our circumcision and crossing over is a renewal of our commitment to our Purpose and Destiny.

You must ensure that you do not drown at your river of circumcision by rejecting the painful circumcision and jumping into the river with all your excess and strange burdens. These will drown you for sure because your ability to successfully cross that river is after the cutting away and offloading of everything that has sought to weigh you down and make you heavy laden.

Surrendering and succumbing to your painful circumcision is what qualifies you to be a transformed vessel of strength, power and dignity and thereby making you a candidate fit to fulfil Destiny.

This symbolic circumcision will require, a breaking up of our "camp of comfort zone", and doing away with the entrenched practices and habits, that we got used to on the other side of the river, in order for us to embrace the right habits that are Destiny oriented.

d. **How to survive and thrive at your river of circumcision**

The circumcised heart and mind is more productive, which enhances your ability to fulfil your Calling and Destiny.

The cutting is a kind of pruning that removes hindrances so as to boost our growth and development, meaning that the circumcision is a process that creates room for greater growth and development.

You will survive the river of circumcision by surrendering to the circumcision, otherwise any attempt to cross over without circumcision will cause you to drown because of the excesses and baggage you are carrying.

You will thrive because when you allow pruning and cutting, it leads to your greater growth, fruitfulness and productivity.

Destiny Questions to Ponder On

1. *Have you ever experienced a **wrestling** and how did it benefit your ability to fulfil your Calling and Destiny?*

2. *Have you ever experienced a **den of despair** and how did it benefit your ability to fulfil your Calling and Destiny?*

3. *Have you ever experienced a **labour of deceit** and how did it benefit your ability to fulfil your Calling and Destiny?*

4. *Have you ever experienced a **valley of vanity** and how did it benefit your ability to fulfil your Calling and Destiny?*

5. *Have you ever experienced a **river of circumcision** and how did it benefit your ability to fulfil your Calling and Destiny?*

6. *Have you ever experienced an **altar of idols** and how did it benefit your ability to fulfil your Calling and Destiny?*

7. *Have you ever experienced a **crossroad to Damascus moment** and how did it benefit your ability to fulfil your Calling and Destiny?*

Chapter 6

PRINCIPLED FOR DESTINY

Adopting The Codes And Habits That Will Guide You To Destiny

Chapter Preview

1. *Your Daily Habits Will Affect Your Destiny*

2. *Your Actions And Behaviors Will Affect Your Destiny*

3. *Your Work Ethics Will Affect Your Destiny*

4. *Your Personal Values Will Affect Your Destiny*

5. *Your Beliefs And Traditions Will Affect Your Destiny*

6. *Your Personal Code of Ethics Will Affect Your Destiny*

7. *Your Personal Mission Statement Will Affect Your Destiny*

OPENING REMARKS

*"A man without principles is like a ship without a compass, it changes direction with every change of wind." ~ **Samuel Smiles***

Principles are values that guide behaviour, decisions, choices and actions, they are what you believe and live by as your standards of behaviour about what is important in your life e.g. Integrity, compassion and fairness.

Principles are fundamental norms, rules or values that represent what is desirable, good and positive for you and that help you to determine what is right or wrong action or behaviour, so principles are important as they make our behaviour consistent and they benefit us in the long run.

In addition, principles, codes, core-values and ethics are crucial guiding lights in enabling you to remain focused and on the right path and will also enable you to make the right decisions and choices by virtue of the fact that you already know what you believe in and what you adhere to.

When we forget our principles or ignore them, we will be sure to fail because when we are gifted and endowed with passion, ambition etc. only our principles will determine whether we use those assets to do good or bad.

*"**Never value your privileges above your principles or you will lose both.**" ~ **Unknow***

Remember that you are judged by your principles and your moral authority and credibility comes from adhering to timeless principles.

Fulfilling your Purpose and Destiny will require you to adopt certain values and core-values by which you will walk and operate to ensure that you fulfil your Purpose with integrity, dignity and honour. In other words, your end must be justified by your means, because how you get there matters.

Righteousness must be your guiding principle.

You will therefore need to develop the right habits, entrenched trademarks, the traits of an eagle woman, growth points from the pit stops in your journey, cross your river of circumcision towards becoming principled for Destiny.

1.   YOUR DAILY HABITS AFFECT YOUR DESTINY

"Chains of habit are too light to be felt until they are too heavy to be broken." By **Warren Buffett**

It is crucial that you develop and maintain the right habits as you seek to fulfil your Purpose and Destiny. This is because your habits form your actions, your actions form your character and your character forms your Destiny.

A habit is a settled or regular tendency or practice, especially one that is hard to give up; an acquired behaviour pattern regularly followed until it has become almost involuntary.

Consistency in doing whatever you want to make a habit even when you don't feel like or you experience challenges in being consistent but you are persistent.

When you commit to that which you want to make a habit, it means you combine effort with commitment and you form a habit. You can create a schedule to keep commitments. Learn to have clear intentions of forming the good habits and celebrate your small wins.

To break from a bad habit, you need to replace it with a good one by discerning and cutting out what triggers those bad habits and the cues that draw you back to those bad habits.

Join forces with somebody who wants to break from those similar habits and surround yourself with people who live the way you want to live and who can challenge you to break those habits.

Set Goals by changing your mind set in regards to those habits by being open to the consequences if you continue with such and face reality and have reason why you need to quit.

"Habits are formed by repetition of particular acts. They are strengthened by the number of repeated acts. Habits are also broken or weakened, and contrary habits are formed by the repetition of contrary acts." By Mortimer J. Adler

2. YOUR ACTIONS AND BEHAVIORS WILL AFFECT YOUR DESTINY

No matter how skilled, gifted, talented or competent you are for purposes of fulfilling your Purpose and Destiny, if your behaviors are not proper and aligned then it will be very difficult for you to actually fulfil that Purpose and Destiny.

Behavior is the way in which one acts or conducts oneself, especially towards others; the way in which an animal or person behaves in response to a particular situation or stimulus.

Ask yourself what are my goals when I engage in this behavior/ way of thinking, feeling, believing, or acting? In other words, what am I getting out of doing it? Setting a goal helps you to adopt a good behaviour.

Consider whether your relationship with other people and the way you utilize those relationships is that which allows you to continue this behavior, or to stop this behaviour. If a behaviour affects your relationship, then letting go is the way to go.

Always challenge yourself to let go of bad behaviour by believing you can and be intentional in fighting that behaviour, and ask yourself where that behaviour is leading you and see if you can live with the consequences of it. Also ask yourself what you must absorb and adopt to change this behaviour?

"Behaviour is the mirror in which we can display our image." **By Mahatma Gandhi**

3. YOUR WORK ETHICS WILL AFFECT YOUR DESTINY

"Ethics is not definable, is not implementable, because it is not conscious; it involves not only our thinking, but also our feeling." ~ **Valdemar W. Setzer**

Fulfilling your Purpose and Destiny will entail a lot of hard work which inevitably requires some high level of discipline as well as ethical dealing.

Work ethic is a set of values based on the ideals of discipline and hard **work. A strong work ethic** is an important part of being successful in your career. Practicing Punctuality and develop the habit of being on time or early for all appointments.

Developing Professionalism goes beyond a crisp white shirt and tie. It includes your attitude, values, and demeanour including being positive and cordial. Be purposeful about cultivating self-discipline because anything worth achieving takes discipline, practice, staying focused on the long-term goal and not being side-tracked by short-term gratification. Train yourself to be persistent and to follow through on projects. Strive for excellence in your assignments.

"You have to have a work ethic, and you have to be educated in what you're doing. You have to take it seriously. It doesn't mean that everything you do has to be serious. But you've got to have the tools." **By Jakob Dylan**

Using Time Wisely by never leaving that ('till tomorrow) which you can do today, learn to complete assignments on time, and ban procrastination from your life, work on Staying Balanced because having a good work ethic does not mean keeping your eyes glued to your computer monitor. It includes knowing how to take care of yourself. Getting proper sleep. Eating right. Taking time to relax and recharge.

"Choices and decisions must be supported by your passion, resolve and a productive work ethic. If these meet opportunity - your success has finally come!" **By Archibald Marwizi**

4. YOUR PERSONAL VALUES WILL AFFECT YOUR DESTINY

"Surround yourself with people who see your value and remind you of it."

In the course of fulfilling your Purpose and Destiny you will need to make a lot of decisions and choices that may seal or abort your Destiny and having the right values is important so that when you make your decisions you will base them on your values and principles.

Value is the regard that something is held to deserve; the importance, worth, or usefulness of something; value can also be defined as principles or standards of behaviour; one's judgement of what is important in life. Values are the things that are important to us, the characteristics and behaviours that motivate us and guide our decisions. Values are a part of us. They highlight what we stand for. They can represent our unique, individual essence.

Start by listing what you consider as valuable to you and stand by those values and let them guide you in decisions you make. The development of a person's values is influenced by the world around him/her. So, it is important to have positive impacting relationship because bad company ruins good morals.

Values guide our behaviour, providing us with a personal code of conduct. When we honor our personal core values consistently, we experience fulfilment.

"There is no value in life except what you choose to place upon it and no happiness in any place except what you bring to it yourself." By Henry David Thoreau

The rate of insecurity whether personally or socially as lack of value threatens our coexistence in peace and harmony, and crime rate increases when we don't have value for self we can't have value others and so hurt and harm others. This can affect to the level of impacting a nation or a country when our values are corroded. Lack of value affects our relationships with others and leads to unnecessary conflicts.

"The value of life lies not in the length of days, but in the use we make of them ~"By Michel de Montaigne

Create clear guidelines, or rules that you intend to follow when interacting with other people on a day-to-day basis. You might also include definitive personal statements that can serve to remind you of the importance you place on applying your personal code of ethics to your life.

Personal ethics is the **code of ethical** guidelines that guide you in your **personal** and professional life. They often develop from your core values and work ethic into actionable goals used in a variety of challenging situations.

Establish your personal reasons for developing this code. You may want to do it for the purpose of guiding your behavior in day-to-day situations, or to serve as inspiration to help you embody the kind of person you want to be.

Write down the traits that you strongly believe represent you as a person. By determining your traits, you can create a more definite and honest code of ethics.

Imagine individual relationships you have with others and determine what you would like to change about each one. If you work closely with others, determining the quality of your relationships will allow you to create a statement for how you want to maintain or improve them.

Lack of personal ethics leads to lack of self-respect and it may lead to discrimination and abuse, where as a person you experience conflict with your relationships. It also leads to people misusing you, controlling and manipulating you because you have no stand or principles of your own to prevent them.

Without personal codes of ethics you don't have boundaries and therefore you can endanger your own life and hinder healthy relationships

"Action indeed is the sole medium of expression for ethics." By Jane Addams

5. YOUR BELIEFS AND TRADITIONS WILL AFFECT YOUR DESTINY

"If you don't stand for something you will fall for anything." ~ **Gordon A. Eadie**

Depending on our socialization, our environment and the culture in which we grew up, we will grow up with certain beliefs and traditions. It is important to discern which of these beliefs and traditions will negatively impact your Destiny and the ones that will positively impact your Destiny so that you can either reject or adopt them.

A belief is an acceptance that something exists or is true, especially one without proof. Belief is also a state or habit of mind in which trust or confidence is placed in some person or thing, something that is accepted, considered to be true, or held as an opinion. Tradition on the other hand is an inherited, established, or customary pattern of thought, action, or behaviour.

When you stand up for what you believe in, you are your own person. You are in charge of what you do. You get to decide what you want and what you like. Standing for what you believe helps you not to lose your identity. Being authentic and standing for your beliefs takes courage and boldness. When you want to make a difference stand for something worth and don't be moved

You should have conviction in your beliefs, but not blind faith.

It's ok to develop a feeling of uncertainty in your beliefs, just make sure you know both sides of the issue though. Seek to know the other side and get fully informed. It is really difficult to take a stand, and stand up for what you believe if you don't really understand the other side or opposing perspective.

Learn to speak up and speak out, and find your voice on your beliefs.

"To believe in something, and not to live it, is dishonest."
~ Mahatma Gandhi

When something bothers you or detrimentally effects what you stand for, then stand up and take your stance. Know that you have the power to change things going on around you by speaking up.

Learn to change negative beliefs by identifying the beliefs you want to change and understand why you want to change them, then take radical action intentionally.

"Be brave to stand for what you believe in even if you stand alone." ~ Roy T. Bennett

6. YOUR PERSONAL CODE OF ETHICS WILL AFFECT YOUR DESTINY

In your journey to Destiny one of the most important resources you will need is relationships in various areas of your life whether it be in your family, social groups, business, profession, spiritual life etc. and since relationships can be complicated and delicate, you must learn to establish clear terms of engagement as to how you will relate in those relationships so as to enhance your Destiny as opposed to threatening it.

Your terms and codes of engagement will include setting boundaries and other such soft rules between you and those you are relating with so as to maintain respect, avoid abuse and maintain clarity as to expectations as opposed to confusion.

Communication is key in building healthy relationships. Learning to listen before we judge or respond is part of communication.

The tone we use when addressing an issue is also part of communication. Being silent is also a form of communication. we need to be balanced and have other's opinion matter before we cut them out.

Active listening is another way of building healthy relationships. This is where learn to hear what someone is saying and responding effectively. Some form of communication is nonverbal where in active listening we listen by observing the body language, tonal variation and be with or rather empathise with others as we listen to them.

Avoiding a judgemental attitude, being critical of other people's intentions based on past hurt or being defensive and justifying wrong doings when corrected or rebuked is a sign of underlying issues that needs to be dealt with in order to build healthy relationships.

Placing very high demands and expectations on others and expecting them to meet you demands is inviting disappointments and frustrations. Be realistic and let your expectations be attainable so to coexist peacefully and build healthy relationships.

Learning to own up to your own mistakes and take responsibility where need be is a way of building healthy relationships. Avoid blaming other for your own misdoing and challenge yourself to own up and be responsible enough to apologise when you offend others.

Never run from conflicts instead face them head on. Resolving dispute is when we acknowledge that we are not perfect and neither is our peer or colleagues. Give people a benefit of doubt allow them to make mistakes and correct them where need be and also accept to be corrected is a way of establishing healthy relationships.

Avoid threats and ultimatums give room for improvement and show compassion to yourself and others.

"If I knew how a lot of my relationships would have turned out, I never would have gotten involved in them... And I would have missed out on some of the best times in my life."
~ L.A. Witt

7. YOUR PERSONAL MISSION STATEMENT WILL AFFECT YOUR DESTINY

All the above culminate in what is known as a personal mission statement where you lay out in very clear terms what your values, ethics, beliefs, aspirations, goals etc. are.

A personal mission statement will also act as a lighthouse in guiding you to where you want to go.

It defines who you are as a person or as a member of a team, it identifies your Purpose and Calling, it explains how you aim to pursue that Purpose and why it matters so much to you etc.

In summary therefore when we talk of being Principled For Destiny, we are referring to all the above issues and to your ability to fulfil your Destiny in a manner that is worthy and righteous.

Destiny Questions to Ponder on

1. *Which of your daily habits do you think are a hindrance to fulfilling your Destiny?*

2. *What actions and behaviors have threatened to derail your Destiny?*

3. *How have your work ethics enhanced your ability to fulfil your Destiny?*

4. *What factors guided you in establishing your personal values and your personal code of ethics?*

5. *What traditions, cultures and beliefs have you found most inconsistent in fulfilling your Purpose and Destiny?*

6. *What difficulties have you encountering in setting terms of engagement in your relationships?*

7. *Do you have a personal mission statement, if not why not?*

Chapter 7

THE SHAPE OF A DESTINY DIAMOND

The Cutting That Will Shape You From The Crown Of Your Head To The Soles Of Your Feet

Chapter Preview

1. **Your Thought patterns**

   (*Aligning your mind-set*)

2. **Your Vision and Sight**

   (*Sharpening your eyes*)

3. **Your Hearing and Listening**

   (*Unclogging your ears*)

4. **Your Speech and Words**

   (*Purifying your mouth*)

5. **Your Emotions and Sentiments**

   (*Purging your motives and agendas*)

6. **Your work and Use of Power**

   (*Cleansing your works and harnessing your power*)

7. **Your walk and lifestyle**

   (*Redirecting your feet*)

OPENING REMARKS

As we embark on our journey to Destiny, we are like raw rough diamonds that need cutting and shaping to unveil and unleash our full potential, value and awesomeness.

Some of the areas in us that are so crucial to our daily functioning are often quite coarse that they threaten our ability to effectively fulfil our Purpose and Destiny and hence the reason they need some refining.

These areas include our thought patterns (our minds), the way we see (our eyes and vision), the way we hear (our ears), the way we speak and use our words (our mouths), the way we feel (our emotions and sentiments), the way we work and exercise our power (our hands), the way we walk and our lifestyle (our feet) etc.

Even after the initial cutting and shaping process the stresses and pressures of daily life take quite a toll on these functionalities and sometimes and unknown to us, they become marred, impaired, sullied, stained, tarnished or blemished and hence the need for regular refining and polishing.

Our ability to surrender to this radical cutting and polishing is an equivocal demonstration of our commitment to our Purpose and Destiny, considering how deeply invasive and incisive the process is.

Suffice that the outcome is worth every cut.

1. YOUR THOUGHT PATTERNS (THE MIND)

If you have an unhealthy fixed mind-set there will need a radical refinement to reframe your mind-set into a mind-set that grows and adjusts accordingly because a fixed mind-set focuses on the negative instead of the positive, hinders growth and hinders potential.

"Nurture your mind with great thoughts, for you will never go any higher than you think." ~ Benjamin Disraeli

Allow yourself to open your mind and let it be flexible, because a fixed mind-set can be changed, and by developing the right beliefs, thoughts, attitude and internalizing and reading the right material and information that is based on what is true, pure and positive.

Also associate with right happy people with positive attitudes and examine your beliefs regularly and erase self-limiting, self-sabotaging thoughts and sieve your thoughts, guard and protect your mind from wrong influences.

"Once your mind-set changes, everything on the outside will change along with it." ~ Steve Maraboli

Once your mind has undergone radical refining, you will have positive thoughts and attitudes. You will see opportunities where you previously saw problems you will operate in a more enthusiastic manner. Your mind will be open to new ideas and concepts, you will be more positive in relating to people and you will be more confident in responding to challenges and obstacles

2. YOUR VISION AND SIGHT (THE EYES)

Eyes symbolize your Vision, your ability to perceive and see sharply, far, wide and deep, meaning that you can see beyond the new and present and visualize ahead, and to see with a wide perception not narrow and to see into things beyond the surface. Your Vision must be powerful, long and sharp to be able to see things and situations in a far reaching and deep way beyond the superficial and shallow.

The most tragic thing is having physical eyesight without inner Vision or ability to have dreams without ideas to pursue and achieve. Those dreams and how and what you see will determine the quality and effectiveness of your Purpose and Destiny.

Your paradigm on people and situations will need to be the correct paradigm otherwise you will fall into errors of judgment bias and prejudice when dealing with them.

Your eyes can become blurred and your Vision compromised due to several factors like past pain, wounded-ness, anger, self-centeredness, greed and all manner of other toxic emotions.

Also, your eyes can get infections which symbolize external contamination from daily seeing, defiled things and the evil in the world, which make your eyes sick.

Another reason for blurred or distorted Vision is allergy. When your eyesight is clouded by misconceptions and biases, and your Vision becomes warped and limited, and distorted. Blurred Vision leads to wrong conclusions and skewed judgments.

Also, a "poor diet". Lack of proper diet, sleep and rest causes poor eyesight and Vision, this means when you feed on the wrong things like reading and watching profanity.

Also "cataracts" which symbolizes issues either from your past or unhealed issues that cloud your ability to see things/ issues subjectively and clearly.

"Short sightedness" is another problem that hinders you or seeing the fine prints that are near thereby missing crucial information and fine details in making your decisions.

Also "long sightedness" that hinders you from seeing far and being a Visionary.

All these defects must therefore be radically refined.

Once your eyes have undergone radical refining, you will see issues sharply and clearly and you will be able to have foresight in seeing the future in respect of the Visions and goals that enable you fulfil your Purpose and Destiny.

In addition, you will be able to scrutinize and discriminate issues more competently. You will be able to see people and issues from a more accurate perspective, to avoid being deceived and being misled. Most importantly you will see and view yourself more accurately without either an inflated sense of self-importance or a distorted sense of worthlessness because good Vision will enable you to be self-aware and balanced.

Like an eagle you will be able to see your enemies from far and also to see oncoming dangers like storms etc. so that you take shelter and protect yourself.

3. YOUR HEARING AND LISTENING (THE EARS)

Your ability to hear clearly and accurately is crucial in your Purpose because you need to hear instructions, well so as to implement and execute them and more importantly to distinguish between the many voices within and around you.

You must learn to hear even the unspoken, so your ears must be sharp and clear. Your hearing is closely intertwined with your actions because you cannot act properly and fully that which you have not heard properly and fully.

"Listen with curiosity. Speak with honesty. Act with integrity. The greatest problem with communication is we don't listen to understand. We listen to reply. When we listen with curiosity, we don't listen with intent to reply. We listen for what's behind the words" ~Roy T. Bennett

Defective ears will cause you not to hear things properly or to imagine what you are hearing or to deflect what you are hearing or to impose your own projections into what you are hearing, or even hearing what you want to hear.

When your ears are clogged and blocked because of listening to wrong things like negative talk, gossip etc. symbolizing dirt and faith that clogging hinders and prevents you from hearing the right things that you need to hear.

Apart from being clogged and blocked with wrong things, your ears may be infected because of careless handling of your ears. When you insert dangerous objects into your ears, it further obstructs your hearing properly. Such objects symbolize, harmful and dangerous information and propaganda likely to derail you from the right path of truth in your Calling. Also associating yourself with the wrong people who are either your enemies and killers of your Vision and Destiny or who pretend to be with you but are not or others who are neither for or against you. Where defamatory and negative reports are spoken about you and your Visions by virtue of being in that environment and conversation, your ears get defiled and infected which may affect your heart towards your Vision (because of that negative information which you now find difficult to erase or forget).

You should radically reject, erase and uproot every dirty and filthy negative information and talk that you have allowed to contaminate, infect and afflict your ears. This can only be done by listening to that which is pure, true, sincere, motivational, uplifting and edifying. Replace the contamination and by radically cutting out every association in your life that causes you to listen to dirt, filth, falsity and negativity (especially about yourself and your Vision or those you love and respect and their Visions). Purposefully and intentionally sieve what you allow yourself to hear and the company you choose to keep.

These radical refinements will of course be painful and uncomfortable because it may mean losing emotional relationships that you are attached to and refraining from going to places and engaging in activities that give you pleasure, but you must for the sake of your Purpose and Destiny.

You will then develop the highest form of listening called emphatic listening which Author Steve Covey has outlined very well in his masterpiece *The 7 Habits of a Highly Effective Person* and it means to seek first to understand what the other person is saying before you seek to be understood. It means when one listens with the intent to understand how the speaker is feeling and understanding their ideas. You develop emphatic listening meaning that you show empathy by identifying with a person's emotions and situation even if you may not be in agreement with them.

"The art of conversation is the art of hearing as well as being heard" ~William Hazlitt

4. YOUR SPEECH AND WORDS (THE MOUTH)

"Remember not only to say the right thing in the right place, but far more difficult still, to leave unsaid the wrong thing at the tempting moment." ~Benjamin Franklin

Your words and speech will need to be refined so that you handle your mouth very wisely. Guard every word you utter, to ensure that no idle or unprofitable words proceeds from your mouth because any misuse of your mouth will reflect negatively on you.

The tongue is a crucial determinant of Destiny, so also learn to tame your tongue as you manage your mouth because a woman with a defective mouth is like a volcano waiting to erupt.

Perhaps the following elements and safeguards will help you in managing your mouth taming your tongue and weighing your words.

What is the content you are about to release? Is it necessary, or relevant? Will it add value to the hearers?

Avoid careless talk where one fails to sieve their words. This makes the mouth smelly, causing foul breath which symbolizes unwholesome and hurtful talk. It's okay not to talk if your content is not wholesome.

Be sensitive about your environment when you talk. Do not talk, at the wrong place. This symbolizes an inability to discern where you should open your mouth and where you should not. Check who is in your surroundings.

Test the timing. When one talks, the timing of one's words is critical. Check if it's the right timing for you and for hearers emotionally, mentally and in terms of other circumstances.

Check your Purpose, reasons and motivations for talking – check your 'why' and 'when'. Don't talk without checking whether it's necessary.

Heed your hearers. Who; when one talks to the wrong people or in the presence of wrong people. Words that may be appropriate to one kind of person may severely wound and damage another person. Some people may have the ability to guard in confidence what is spoken to them while others may not have that ability.

"Let's acknowledge the difference between speaking up with intention and speaking up for attention." ~Monica Lewinsky

Alter your attitude. How one talks; the tone, volume, body posture and facial expression.

Proverbs 18:21 – "Death and life are in the power of the tongue, and those who love it will eat its fruit."

Radically scrape out all foul talk and speech with the sword namely the word of God by using your mouth to read and speak the words that edify and build up others.

Radically Rinse your mouth with prayer, praise and worship and pure sincere, relevant talk Seasoned with truth and grace in order to eradicate the foul smell and breath

Radically Bandage your heart with grace, peace, patience, kindness etc. because your mouth speaks from the abundance of your heart

Let your heart guard your mouth as regards its motives.

Radically discriminate, sieve who to associate with so as to guard who to talk to

Radically put a hot coal on your lips and scourge them like Isaiah the prophet as a reminder to speak only that which is right and pure.

Radically pluck yourself from people of unclean lips so as to overcome all evil speech.

Once you allow the radical refining of your mouth, you will marvel at how a healed mouth is a very powerful and useful tool and weapon in the hand of a faithful Destiny runner because that mouth will release words that set the course for your life towards Destiny and after the mouth has undergone radical surgery, you will learn to be a person of few words to **listen more** and **talk less**.

"A good speech should be like a woman's skirt; long enough to cover the subject and short enough to create interest." ~ Winston S. Churchill

Your refined and healed mouth will utter words that are Seasoned with grace and wisdom and a mouth that consults with your mind and your heart so as to think carefully before talking, so that you can be trusted to remain confidential and to guard the welfare of those you speak to and on behalf of.

5. YOUR EMOTIONS AND SENTIMENTS (THE HEART)

The heart bears burdens, agendas, motives and emotions whether positive or negative. The condition of the heart is very crucial because it affects and determines what comes out of the mouth.

In the physical and natural a heart attack is when some arteries in your body that supply your heart with vital life blood get blocked and clogged up because of undesirable deposits or harmful substances. Likewise, when you allow toxic emotions in your life, they block and clog the right things coming to your heart which symbolizes an emotional "heart attack."

Your heart can become defiled and contaminated by all manner of toxic emotions.

- **Bitterness, jealousy** and envy arising from resentments in situations for example when other people are promoted and you are not or they are performing better than you.
- **Anger and offence** where you develop fits of rage from uncontrolled emotions and you allow offences to become a snare and to obstruct and cloud your judgement and cause you to be vindictive.
- **Hurt & woundedness** and past pain which you refuse to release and heal from and you develop a self-pity victim syndrome which paralyzes you.
- **Disappointments** and frustrations arising from feelings of not being appreciated or receiving the rewards you expect or achieving the goals you aimed for.
- **Selfish ambitions**, motives and agendas – where you harbour selfishness, seeking your own interests before the interests of others.
- **Hatefulness**, harshness and unkindness caused by your mistrust of people and inability to develop healthy relationships during the course of your journey.

At this point you need radical refinements of your heart to avoid a "heart failure."

Humble yourself and acknowledge that you are harbouring these toxic issues in your heart, and seek the reasons why and what caused them, so that you can uproot them.

Put your pride aside and address and confront each issue radically, cut them and uproot them from your heart.

Replace negative toxic emotions with their antidotes namely: forgiveness, love, patience, kindness and for bearance etc.

Remain self-aware so that you can sense when any of those toxic emotions try to invade you and keep your heart surrounded with positive feelings so that there will be no room for the negative ones.

Once the heart has undergone a radical refining you will harbour sincere selfless motives agendas and feelings and emotions that are healthy so that you will forgive easily and show kindness, patience, love and tolerance. Once you have been healed of past pain, woundedness and grief, you will be able to develop and maintain healthier relationships and you will generally be more passionate and enthusiastic in the fulfilment of your Purpose and Destiny.

Develop coping mechanisms against negative emotions by surrounding yourself with positive people and submit yourself to loving counselling and mentorship.

"A man sees in the world what he carries in his heart." ~ Johann Wolfgang von Goethe

6. YOUR WORK AND USE OF POWER (THE HANDS)

Fulfilling your Purpose and Destiny is hard work and commitment and your hands Symbolize work, diligence, work ethics, and power. So, when your work and performance is below par and your use of the power at your disposal in questionable and abusive then your hands need a radical refining.

Broken hands; meaning weakness and unable to do hard work.

Lazy hands symbolize unwilling to work and poor work ethics.

Weak hands; means doubt, procrastination in your work.

Defiled hands; meaning handling unclean things and taking bribes, unjust gains and corruption.

High handedness; meaning misuse of power, lording it over people, whereby you exploit and oppress people.

If you find yourself manifesting any of the above symptoms;

- **Fix your broken hands** by realigning the broken bones meaning rechecking your values and character issues. Healed hands means that your strength is restored and you become empowered for your Purpose and destroy.
- **Cleanse your defiled hands** by turning away from all dishonest dealings and use your power maturely.

Abuse of power is often a sign of immaturity and it also shows that you were not ready for it that you were not ready for it or that you have an identity crisis. When we are secure in our identity we lead and exercise power with maturity and sensitivity and the power does not go to our heads.

Once your hands undergo a radical refinement and you are set free from laziness and lethargy, you will have stronger hands and be more productive and fruitful. You will operate with the right values and good work ethics and you will develop self-motivation and an increased energy for fulfilling your Purpose. Importantly you will develop temperaments compassion, respect and moderation in handling people instead of being high handed.

Maintaining healthy refined hands will require you to intentionally develop good work ethics by studying how to develop solid core-values and principles and adhere to them and allow them to guide in your every decision and action.

"Work ethic is the most important component of being successful"
~Kliff Kingsbury

7. YOUR WALK AND LIFESTYLE (THE FEET)

Prov.4:26 "Ponder the path of your feet, and let all your ways be established."

Feet symbolize someone's walk and lifestyle, your value habits and behaviour, codes and principles and your ability to move forward, progress advance and accomplish milestones in fulfilling your Purpose and Destiny. So, you need to have healthy feet because feet also symbolize your obedience in going where you are sent or posted.

Feet also symbolize your ability to be stable and grounded in your place of Purpose and also your walk and lifestyle in terms of your morals and character, hallmarks and trademarks. The washing of feet also symbolizes servanthood (as Jesus taught), meaning that when our walk and lifestyle is upright then we are more likely to operate very effectively with a servant's heart.

The feet also symbolize possessing and taking authority over territories and situations, when we step into those territories and situations.

"The place where you made your stand never mattered. Only that you were there…. And still on your feet." ~ Stephen King

When, your walk and lifestyle are questionable in terms of your honesty and integrity. When you become disobedient by not going where you are sent or posted or by not being stable and grounded in your place of Purpose (or when your feet are hasty to take you to the wrong places) then it means your feet have become defective and your ability to serve effectively will be greatly prejudiced.

"Be sure you put your feet in the right place, then stand firm." ~ Abraham Lincoln

- **"Lame feet"** means an inherent defect one is born with, causing one not to walk straight. It means that it is hereditary from one's history and ancestors and it is a generational issue passed through the genes.

  This could symbolizes a dishonest walk and lifestyle that one has inherited or picked up from their family background where perhaps your parents or relatives were also dishonest and lacked integrity in their walk and life and which affected their ability to serve effectively.

  Walking straight means having good morals, honesty and integrity so inability to walk straight means a crooked walk and lifestyle that is dishonest without integrity.

- **"Crippled or disabled"** meaning broken or maimed accidentally causing someone to walk but with difficulty.

  Being crippled or disabled through accident could symbolize that though you do not deliberately or intentionally choose to have crippled or disabled feet (walk and lifestyle), none the less there are actions, decisions and choices you have made that are causing your walk and lifestyle to be crippled and disabled by your mistakes and poor choices.

  Walking with difficulty therefore could symbolize that though you are walking, you are not being able to do so effectively and thereby though you are fulfilling your Purpose, you are doing so with difficulty and therefore not effectively.

- **'Heavy set feet'** making you slow in movement either due to wearing wrong footwear or due to wrong use of the feet or lack of exercise that causes the feet to be heavy causing you to lag behind without proper progress and advancement.

The heaviness symbolizes laziness and lethargy;

The wrong foot wear symbolizes lack of proper understanding and information and lack of the proper equipment and tools required in your Purpose

Wrong use of feet symbolizes being at the wrong place at the wrong time.

Lack of exercise symbolizes a lack of proper habits that will enable you to develop consistency and discipline which will make your journey light and expeditious.

- **"Cold feet"** symbolizes a lack of courage, being indecisive and procrastination in your walk and lifestyle thereby hindering effective service. Cold feet also symbolize one who has an unstable mind and thereby changes his mind hastily and carelessly.

With these shortcomings and feet issues, you definitely need a radical refining of your walk and lifestyle.

For **"lame feet"** you will need to brace and align the feet (walk and lifestyle) to give the required support in terms of accountability relationships, co-values and good work ethics to enable you serve effectively.

Putting on braces to support your lame or crippled feet symbolizes having the right relationships, core-values and work ethics.

For **"Crippled and Disabled feet"** there will be need to have the crippled bones corrected so as to replace the disability with ability. This symbolizes correcting your actions, decisions, choices and habits so that your walk and lifestyle become properly enabled and empowered as opposed to being disabled.

For **"Heavyset feet"** will need to be unburdened and lightened in order to acquire a swiftness and speed symbolizing that once you adopt the right habits, empower yourself with understanding and knowledge as regards your service so that you are able to serve expeditiously and energetically.

For **"Cold feet"** they will require to be warmed up symbolizing you'll need to develop self-confidence and a secure **identity** and courage to enable you be proactive in making your decisions and stable in your mind.

Once your feet (walk and lifestyle) have undergone a radical surgery, you will develop good morals and good values. You will become accountable as regards your lifestyle, walk and journey.

Your integrity will be restored and you will develop an ability to go to the right places at the right time, because you will walk upright with integrity and truth without being bent over and crippled and without compromising and being economical with the truth.

You will become **solidly grounded** in your place of Purpose. You will wear the right foot wear (having the right equipment, understanding and tools for your assignment, Purpose and Destiny.)

"Keep your feet on the ground and your thoughts at lofty heights."
~ Peace Pilgrim

Learn to surrender to these radical cuttings, refinements and polishing's for the sake of your Purpose and Destiny and as you allow the "Diamond" within you to be unveiled.

Destiny Questions to Ponder On

1. *What aspects of your **mind/thought pattern/attitude** do you think needs **refining** and why?*

2. *What aspects of your **eyes/Vision/sight** do you think needs **refining** and why?*

3. *What aspects of your **ears/hearing/listening** do you think needs **refining** and why?*

4. *What aspects of your **mouth/words/speech** do you think needs **refining** and why?*

5. *What aspects of your **heart/emotions** do you think needs **refining** and why?*

6. *What aspects of your **hands/work/power** do you think needs **refining** and why?*

7. *What aspects of your **feet/walk/lifestyle** do you think needs **refining** and why?*

This Page Was Intentionally Left Blank

Chapter 8

THE TRADEMARKS OF A DESTINY VESSEL

Branding Your Uniqueness for Effectiveness

Chapter Preview

OPENING REMARKS

"You will be a vessel for honourable use, set apart as holy and useful to the master of the house ready for every good work." ~ **Unknown**

In the journey to Destiny there are many vessels some **headed towards** Destiny and some **headed away** from Destiny, and the question as to what kind of a vessel you are, is determined by the presence or absence of certain hallmarks and trademarks in your life, so that you become a vessel with substance.

"The empty vessel makes the loudest sound." ~ **William Shakespeare.**

Some of the most significant hallmarks and trademarks you will possess as a vessel of a Destiny, are to be found in the word D.E.S.T.I.N.Y.

"You are God's chosen vessel in which the treasure of His power resides." ~ **Pst. Sean Rajapakse.**

The "D" says that you are dignified.

The "E" says that you are of an excellent spirit and attitude,

The "S" says that you are a woman of strength,

The "T" says that you are tenacious,

The "I" says that you are a woman of **integrity,**

The "N" says that you are **noble**, and

The "Y" says that you are **yielded.**

1. A VESSEL OF DIGNITY

Proverbs 31:25 – *"Strength and honor are her clothing; she shall rejoice in time to come."*

There are two types of dignity, firstly the type of dignity that is fake and forced on and secondly the type of dignity that drapes itself around you automatically by virtue of your distinguished character.

To fulfil your Purpose and Destiny you must have a healthy measure of dignity in the sense that you must always carry yourself as one who is worthy of honour and respect in a composed manner and style so that no matter how stressful a situation is and no matter how much pressure you are under, you will have the ability to stand strong and tall in the face of adversity.

Suffice to say, that your dignity should enhance and not hinder your ability to fulfil Destiny.

Always keeping in mind that it is your right to be valued and respected for your own sake and to be treated ethically by those around you.

"Human dignity is the most important right from which all other fundamental rights derive." ~ **Unknown**

For you a woman of Destiny, your standard, must be higher than normal in the sense that even where your right to dignity is breached, you will not retaliate or respond in an in dignified manner, in other words never allow the dignity of others to defile or contaminate your own dignity.

Yet being dignified does not mean allowing others to walk all over you, it is taking a firm stand for your beliefs and values, but without closing your mind to the views and opinions of others. It goes without saying that even as you have a right to be treated with dignity, you must also treat others with dignity.

"Become a dignitary by treating others with dignity." ~ (Bryant McGill)

In the course of fulfilling your Destiny you will inevitably come across situations where no matter how hard you try you will lose your dignity or your right to dignity will be stepped on.

At that point it will be your responsibility to regain your dignity by forgiving yourself and others, and taking steps to re-instate broken boundaries, and undertakings so that you may move on without delaying or prejudicing your Purpose and Destiny.

1 Peter 2:17 *"Honour all people. Love the brotherhood. Fear God. Honour the king."*

2. A VESSEL OF EXCELLENCE

"Excellence is not a skill; it is an attitude." ~ **Ralph Marston.**

Fulfilling your Purpose and Destiny, is one thing but fulfilling it well is another thing. Your input in anything has a range from poor, average to excellence and as a true woman of Destiny it is important to choose to be excellent, distinct and superior in everything you put your hand to by harnessing your brilliance and achieving mastery.

"Excellence is to do a common thing in an uncommon way" ~ **Steve Jobs.**

Never settle for less than you are capable of, or less than you can be or less than what you are entitled to.

Mediocrity is a very loathsome word to real woman of Destiny and you must never be associated with it. Having a spirit of excellence is becoming outstanding and a mark of distinction and virtue as a never-ending process.

"Excellence is the gradual results of always striving to do better." **~Pat Riley.**

Excellence demonstrates your commitment to being truly the best that you can be and bringing out the best you. The best you will automatically produce and the best quality of anything you do. It means refusing to settle for good, when you know you have the spirit of excellence within you. Good enough is not your Destiny because you were created for excellence.

"Excellence is never an accident; it is the result of high intention, sincere effort, intelligent direction, skillful execution, and the Vision to see obstacle as opportunity." ~ **Anonymous.**

Always aim to achieve excellence in everything you do, by having a strong hunger desire, a passion for it, emulating role models of excellence, so you bench mark against the best, planning well and working hard, and choosing quality.

"The will to win, the desire to succeed, the urge to reach your full potential, these are the keys that will unlock the door to personal excellence." ~ **Confucius.**

3. A VESSEL OF STRENGTH

"Strong women wear their pain like stilettos. No matter how much it hurts, all you see is the beauty of it." ~ **Harriet Morgan**

Fulfilling your Purpose and Destiny is not for the faint hearted, and it will require you to be strong in all dimensions;

Physically by taking care of your body;

Emotionally by constantly eliminating toxic emotions, guarding your heart against and ensuring that you harbour pure and right emotions;

Mentally by pulling down and casting out every negative thought pattern that seeks to become a stronghold in your mind, and instead adopting a positive thought pattern by dwelling on that which is true and healthy for your mind;

Spiritually by meditating on and keeping what is pure and true in your heart, remaining in constant fellowship with brethren and seeking a closer relationship with God prayer.

Proverbs 18:10 – *"The name of the LORD is a strong tower; the righteous run to it and are safe."*

The journey to Destiny will take its toll on you for sure, and you will undergo harsh storms and vicious attacks in every area of your life to the point where you will become severely weakened and vulnerable, which will seriously prejudice your ability to fulfil your Purpose. So, you must resolve to intentionally strengthen yourself and remain strong to survive and thrive.

*"Whenever you find yourself doubting how far you can go, just remember how far you have come. Remember everything you have faced, all the battles you have won, and all the fears you have overcome." ~ **N.R. Walker***

Strength is developed through your struggles, storms, hardships, conflict, battles, failing and falling and by overcoming all these adversities even though you thought you couldn't.

"You were given this life because you are strong enough to live it."
~ Nishan Panwar

4. A VESSEL OF TENACITY

"Tenacity is the ability to hang on when letting go appears most attractive." ~ Unknown

Tenacity is crucial hallmark and trademark of a woman of Destiny because quitting and giving up will be a constant temptation that will taunt you. The only way to avoid giving in to these temptations, will be your ability to grip your Purpose and Destiny so firmly in your heart and mind with such a firmness of single-mindedness, tireless staying power, and with a bulldog spirit.

"In the journey to success, tenacity of Purpose is supreme." Aliko Dangote

Tenacity is the ability to be so determined and persistent, as if you were swimming across a pool, and you know that any faltering, wavering or a slackening of your strokes, will lead to inevitable drowning in the miry waters of oblivion.

Your tenacity as you fulfil your Purpose will often be misunderstood as foolish stubbornness and hardness to those around, you, who do not have a revelation of what it takes to fulfil Purpose. So, you must not be derailed, nor loosen your grip, by the misguided perception of others.

"Tenacity is setting a goal so BIG you can't possibly achieve it... then growing to the person who can." ~ Unknown

The giants and forces seeking to hinder you from fulfilling your Purpose cannot be confronted by a polite will but by the strength of will like no other. A tenacious woman is one who values her Destiny so she lays hold of it with a tight grip from the forces seeking to wrench it out of her.

Ephesians 4:1 *"I, therefore, the prisoner of the Lord, beseech you to walk worthy of the Calling with which you were called."*

5.   A VESSEL OF INTEGRITY

"Integrity lies in, doing what one speaks; speaking what one does."
~M. K. Soni

Your ability to be honest and have strong moral values in the midst of a morally decadent society, and to have sound work and business ethics in the midst of a corrupt and crocked market place. Your ability to walk in uprightness, accountability and responsibility and a consistency and refusal to compromise on what you hold true and right, are non-negotiable hallmarks and trademarks of a woman of Destiny, because your integrity is the foundation of your character.

Prov.11:3 – *"The integrity of the upright will guide them, but the perversity of the unfaithful will destroy them."*

Needless to say, developing and maintaining integrity as you fulfil your Purpose is a personal responsibility that you cannot delegate or rest from.

"Integrity is choosing your thoughts and actions based on values rather than personal gain." ~ **Chris Karcher**

If you cannot be honest with people, you cannot develop long-term meaningful relationships with them, because there is no trust.

If you are not honest with yourself... if you violate your own values, you will have difficulty trusting yourself. You will eventually become overwhelmed with doubt, and with good reason.

If you do not have values, or have them but do not hold to them, you will have difficulty knowing how you will act when tough choices arise in life.

6. A NOBLE VESSEL

*"True nobility isn't about being better than someone else. It is about being better than the 'you', you used to be." ~ **Wayne W. Dyer***

As a Destiny vessel and having endured your share of adversity in your journey, you will come to a place, when you can honestly make claim to being "a noble vessel."

Being noble entails having or showing fine personal qualities high moral eminence, upright and decent, free from anything petty or dubious.

*"There are just two things that can make you famous... being noble or notorious." ~ **Ram Mohan***

The wife of **noble character** in **Proverbs 31** is defined by her ability to make smart choices by seeking wisdom that comes from God, among other things like virtue, strength, industrious who loves and serves etc.

As a noble vessel, you inspire confidence in others, work to increase people's values, always focusing on the good. Your dress code of conduct is fearing the lord, and becomes a credible model for others to emulate because of the way you carry yourself even in the most difficult situation.

*"A noble person overcomes troubles with dignity." ~ **Confucius***

Noble qualities are crucial in a leadership role by virtue of the magnitude of people you are influencing and to that extent, being beyond reproach, inspiring confidence, trust and hope for those you are leading. You are to keep above strife, corruption and injustices etc. Such things are beneath a noble woman.

*"A noble leader answers not the trumpet calls of self-promotion, but to the hushed whispers of necessity." ~**Mollie Marti***

Purpose to be a noble vessel as you fulfil your Purpose and Destiny, because it is how you finish and finishing well is noble.

7. A YIELDED VESSEL

*"God is not looking for gold vessels or silver vessels. He is looking for yielded vessels." ~ **Kathryn Kuhlman***

Your ability to balance your strength and tenacity with a humble yieldedness is a crucial trademark and hallmark, because it speaks to your maturity and wisdom in being able to be obedient, submitted, and pliable.

"Obedience is yielding more readily to one who commands gently."
*~ **Seneca***

Contrary to popular belief your yieldedness is not a sign of weakness but rather a sign of strength because it shows that you are not narrow minded and petty, stubbornly sticking to your position, and views when it is no longer tenable or logical.

"If you can't be flexible in life, you become irritable with life." ~
Rubyanne.

Being yielded helps you to master the art of negotiation in remaining open to the interests of the other party and seeking a win-win outcome for the mutual benefit of all. This is as opposed to demanding only what is best for you to the prejudice and destruction of the other party. You have to maintain healthy relationships characterized by respect, honour and selflessness.

"Why is it when you yield, I feel like the one who has been conquered?" **Judith McNaught**

Lastly and perhaps most importantly is that yieldedness enables you to humbly accept your mistakes and rectify them speedily to avoid unnecessary delays in your journey. It also makes you teachable in accepting and addressing your weaknesses and shortcomings, so as to avoid self-sabotage.

"Being yielded to God's authority keeps us pliable and open-minded to possible change of plans." **Beth Moore**

Yieldedness goes beyond service and physical action and it involves the condition of your heart and mind. It may entail giving up possessions, rights or claims, relinquishing control over something to another, or giving up a position of advantage or privilege, where necessary. This means that being yielded may not be an option for a Destiny woman but a requirement.

Destiny Questions to Ponder On

1. *In which order would you prioritize these trademarks? (i.e., in order of the most necessary)*

2. *Which of these trademarks do you believe you possess and why?*

3. *Which trademarks do you think you have not yet developed within you and why?*

4. *Which of these trademarks have proved most challenging for you to operate in?*

5. *Which of these trademarks do you think you can do without and still fulfil your Destiny?*

6. *Which one trademark do you believe has empowered you most?*

7. *Which one trademark do you think has not added much value in your fulfilling your Destiny?*

This Page Was Intentionally Left Blank

Chapter 9

THE HABITS OF A DESTINY ADDICT

Building Better Habits to Unlock Your

Greatness

Chapter Preview

1. *Harnessing your brilliance*

2. *Doing regular reality checking*

3. *Mastering time management*

4. *Prudent preparation*

5. *Recovering speedily*

6. *Life balancing*

7. *Praying fervently*

OPENING REMARKS

"Your habits will determine your future." ~ Jack Canfield

In the course of fulfilling your Purpose and Destiny you will need to develop certain habits that will make you effective and efficient. Good habits will enable you to remain on course, and focused and will make your journey smoother and less stressful.

"Successful people are simply those with successful habits." ~Brian Tracy

Adhering to good habits reaps a good character and a good character ultimately reaps a Destiny.

Good habits such as harnessing your brilliance regular reality checks, managing your time critically, being ruthless with prudent preparation, having an ability to recover speedily and failing forward towards your goals as well as your ability to manage and maintain a healthy life balance in all areas of your life plus consistent fervent prayer and Destiny will greatly equip you in fulfilling your Purpose.

"We first make our habits then our habits make us." ~ John Dryden

Your success will be found in your daily routine.

Habits can either be a positive or a negative settled and regular tendency and practice, pattern, routine behaviours whether conscious or unconscious, formed by regular repetition.

"Chains of habit are too light to be felt until they are too heavy to be broken." ~Warren Buffet

Understanding how your habits affect you and your ability to fulfil your Purpose and Destiny will help you choose which habits to break and reject and which ones to adopt and embrace.

*"Depending on what they are, our habits will either make or break us. We become what we repeatedly do." ~ **Sean Covey***

You can break your bad habits by replacing them with good habits. Sometimes we may be so bound by bad habits that we begin to justify them. We begin to lose perspective as to what are good and bad habits and without an ability to identify good habits and bad habits, means you will not have the motivation to change what is bad.

*"Bad habits are like a bed easy to get in but hard to get out of." ~ **Unknown***

Good habits are recognized by the results you are getting from any area of your life, for example success in business, healthy fulfilling relationships etc. Obviously if results are negative and undesirable and then the habit is bad.

*"Good or bad, habits always deliver results." ~ **Jack Canfield***

1. HARNESSING YOUR BRILLIANCE

As a woman of Destiny, you must know and understand that there is a wealth of brilliance within you in terms of gifting, soft skills, hard skills, talents, potential and quality character traits etc. These should not lie dormant but must be harnessed in order to make you productive, fruitful, and profitable to maximize your ability and empower you to fulfil your Purpose and Destiny.

"I don't care how much power, brilliance or energy you have, if you don't harness it and focus it on specific target and hold it there, you are never going to accomplish as much as your ability warrants." ~Zig Ziglar

In addition, there is passion, emotions, mental ability, excellence, energy, commitment and zeal within you that must also be harnessed in order to bring them under your control and proper use and for maximum benefit. You have the brilliance of a fine diamond that is precious and valuable for your use and profit.

*"Open your eyes and see the brilliance within. It's there waiting for you to notice. Just give it a try." ~**Unknown***

Consequently, as a wise woman you will ensure that you constantly and consistently keep harnessing that brilliance without allowing it to become dull or dormant. You must ensure this in every area of your life (whether it be in your business, profession, social capital, spiritual walk, family enterprises, your personal Visions and projects etc.)

Harnessing your ability to master the art of self-discipline is crucial to your ability to fulfil your Purpose. Self-discipline comes at a great personal cost and it is a choice you make deliberately and intentionally without the need of anyone forcing you so it is voluntary and you hold yourself accountable for your actions.

Harnessing your brilliance will also require you to be proactive meaning that you must have the ability to take action effectively to self-improve and always be ahead of the game. Proactivity is also the ability to take responsibility for your choices, actions and growth and the unleashing of your full potential.

2. DOING REGULAR REALITY CHECKING

*"The truth does not change according to your ability to stomach it." ~ **Flannery O'Connor***

One of the things that can hinder you from progressing effectively and successfully in fulfilling your Purpose and Destiny is a failure to see yourself, people issues and situations etc. as they really are. Beware of remaining in denial over crucial issues so that you end up operating at a limited measure without sufficient real knowledge, information and revelation and thereby failing to meet your mark or failing to accomplish your goals and Visions effectively.

Some of the areas of your life where a constant reality check is needful are for example;

- **In your finances** to avoid collapsing financially because of naïve, careless and uninformed decisions.

- **In your relationships** in order to really know who is who in your life, what is their value and relevance as well as your expectations and their expectations in that relationship?

- **In your parenting,** because it enables you to see exactly who your child is, and where they are at, as opposed to seeing only what you want to see. To help you acknowledge and confront dysfunctions that could ruin his or her life as opposed to remaining in denial until the damage done is irreparable.

- **In your Calling,** a constant reality check is also needed to assess your progress or lack of it, to determine where you are at vis-à-vis where you need to be, so that you can make the necessary adjustments to remain on course and ensure that your visions have not become distorted or derailed.

- **In your adverse situations;** the courage to avoid burying your head in the sand about the actual reality of your adverse circumstances and learning to confront those brutal facts squarely in order to deal with them effectively.

Facing your current reality at any time of your life is crucial but you must do so without losing your faith.

"If you change the way you look at things, the things you look at will change." ~ **Dr. Wayne Dyer.**

A reality check entails receiving correct and honest information, conducting autopsies and allowing people to give you feedback, which you can sieve and sift and apply what fits and works.

So, Purpose to intentionally change any reality that does not align with your Destiny. Your daily confessions and affirmations, your decrees and declarations, should align with your goals and visions. Practice positive self-talk, write and commit to a personal mission statement. Create the reality you want and need to fulfil your Destiny.

"Let your dreams change your reality, don't let your reality change your dreams." ~ **Amanda Redwood**

3. MASTERING TIME MANAGEMENT

"Time management is life management." ~ **Unknown**

Time is one currency that you can never get back once it is gone so managing your time, developing punctuality in your appointments and using your time wisely is a habit you will have to develop and walk in.

Avoiding distractions, time wasters, saying NO to carrying other peoples' monkeys, tracking how you have spent your time at the end of each day, prioritizing and delegating that which others can do for you are crucial time management skills that everyone needs.

*"Time is your most precious gift because you only have a set amount of it. You can make more money, but you can't make more time. When you give someone your time, you are giving them a portion of your life that you'll never get back." ~ **Rick Warren***

Study time management principles, invest in appropriate seminars. Watch successful people who have learnt to master time. Your journey to Destiny is a continuous learning curve.

Psalm 90:12 *"So teach us to number our days, that we may gain a heart of wisdom."*

You must become the **"master of your** minutes."

Beware, because if you fail to manage and own your time, people will do it for you and once you lose time you risk losing your Destiny.

*"Your time is your most valuable coin in your life. You and you alone will determine how that coin will be spent. Be careful that you do not let other people spend it for you." ~ **Carl Sandburg.***

4. PRUDENT PREPARATION

"Proper preparation prevents poor performance." ~ Charlie Batch

Planning and preparing is a sequence of action steps to achieve some specific goal. Effective planning and preparation reduces the time required for execution. Fulfilling your Purpose will entail thoughtful and careful preparation and planning and to that extent you will need to be organized and structured and ready to do all that it takes to ensure that you are well equipped for your Purpose.

The French call it *"mis en place,"* a culinary phrase which means putting in place, setting up all the ingredients required before cooking.

Preparing for any situation, task or assignment whether it be a simple as preparing a meal for your family or as grand as launching a mega-Vision will require ruthless, deliberate and intentional preparation keeping in mind that proper preparation is the foundation for excellent execution.

"Failing to prepare is preparing to fail." ~ **John Woodew**

Prudent and ruthless preparation means mixing wisdom with unbending meticulous excellence and it involves every part of you, namely physically, emotionally, mentally and spiritually because all of you must align for the preparation to be complete.

"A goal without a plan is just a wish." ~ **Antoine de Saint**

Intentional preparation empowers you for whatever comes at you whether good or bad, so that you are well equipped to discern your hour of visitation or your hour of adversity.

Being properly prepared for any task or assignment demonstrates the commitment and seriousness you have for that task and assignment and the value you place upon it vis-à-vis your Purpose and Destiny. Proper physical planning and preparation demonstrates the condition of your mind and heart towards your task. Careless preparation or no planning shows a confused, unprepared mind and heart.

Do not be like the virgins in the bible who were found unprepared and unequipped.

5. RECOVERING SPEEDILY

"Learn to fail fast and forward." **Unknown**

This is when you quickly acknowledge a failure or a mistake, do the necessary damage control and move on. The problem most of us women have is erroneously thinking that we have the luxury of wallowing in self-pity after a failure or that we are entitled to and we should wait for **"sympathy cards,"** before getting up and moving on.

"Success is not final; failure is not fatal; it is the courage to continue that counts." ~ **Winston Churchill.**

Moving on after failure is one thing but the speed with which you move on is another thing.

Failure in itself comes with valuable lessons which you should be eager to put into practice immediately before the pain of your failure suffocates those lessons.

So as a Destiny chaser you must always ensure that recovery from any failure and set back is speedy, so that you do not lose the momentum of your chase.

"There are no mistakes or failures, only lessons." ~*Denis Waitley*

In addition, learning to fail forward not backwards means having no regrets accepting reality and learning from your setbacks.

"Failure should be our teacher, not our undertaker. It's a delay not defeat. It is a temporary detour, not a dead-end street." ~*William A. Ward*

6. LIFE BALANCING

"Balance is not something you find; it is something you create."
~Jana Kingsford.

As a woman of Destiny, you will inevitably have many roles to play in your life whether as a wife, mother, professional, business woman, a leader etc. You will have several multi-tasks to perform and accomplish well, so you will often be stressed and over stretched if you do not learn how to balance effectively and successfully.

Learn to fulfil each role and accomplish each task within its required time span and slot by learning to work smarter not harder and setting clear boundaries between your various roles where necessary.

*"Without balance, a life is no longer worth the effort. ~ **Olen Steinhauer***

A lack of balance will throw you into confusion and turmoil and render your performance mediocre. You may even neglect crucial roles and aspects of your life to your detriment and to the detriment of others who are depending on you.

*"Without balance life is a hot race." ~ **Unknown***

So, whether it be your career, family, health, friends etc. you must create the necessary and right balance.

*"Work is a rubber ball. If you drop it, it will bounce back. The other four balls, family health, friends and integrity are made of glass. If you drop one of these, it will be irrevocably scuffed, nicked, perhaps even shattered." ~ **Gary Keller.***

Life is about balance, be kind but don't let people abuse you. Trust but don't be deceived. Be content but never stop improving yourself.

Setting goals in every area of your life, assessing and evaluating yourself constantly, to ensure you are maintaining a healthy balance. Yet be kind to yourself because, being balanced will not feel good, if you are cruel to yourself in creating it.

"Life is a balance between what you can control and what we cannot control. I am learning to live between effort and surrender." **~ Danielle Orner**

Fulfilling your Purpose and Destiny will entail maintaining a healthy balance in all the various aspects of your life.

Ecclesiastics 3:1-8 – *"To everything there is a season, a time for every purpose under heaven…"*

7. PRAYING FERVENTLY

"A day without prayer is a day without blessing, and a life without prayer is a life without power." **~ Edwin Harvey**

It goes without saying that constant praying enquiring and seeking guidance and directions from God is a mandatory habit that any woman with any chance of fulfilling her Purpose and Destiny must adopt and cultivate.

God is your creator and the one who ordained your Destiny so he knows everything there is to know about that Destiny and failure to constantly consult him is a serious oversight.

"There is no greater discovery than seeing God as the author or your Destiny." **~ Ravi Zacharias**

- **Firstly,** your **"secret place of prayer"** physically, emotionally and mentally is a very powerful and special place where you must retreat daily. Your constant desire once there, should always be to ask for revelation and insight, grace and strength, consistency and fervency, joy and passion.

- **Secondly,** your **"secret place of prayer"** is your altar of prayer, physically or symbolically and sometimes when you neglect the habit of prayer and live in prayerlessness, or you start walking against the will of God, the symbolic altar will begin to disintegrate and break and you must return to it and pray to God to restore the broken altars of prayer in your life.

- **Thirdly,** your **"secret place of prayer"** must have certain elements to keep it powerful and strong, namely a relationship between you and God, an intimate father child walk. There must be continuous sacrifice because prayer is hard work and serious commitment, there must be faith, consistency, fervency and travail from which you will receive revelation and empowerment.

1 John 5:14 – *"Now this is the confidence that we have in Him, that if we ask anything according to His will, He hear us."*

Destiny Questions to Ponder On

1. *In which ways have you been harnessing your brilliance?*

2. *In which specific areas have you had to do regular reality checks and what specific benefits did you see?*

3. *What distractions do you struggle within your attempt to manage your time effectively?*

4. *What factors do you take into considerations when you start to prudently prepare and plan?*

5. *How have you ensured speedy recovery from your failures and setbacks?*

6. *What measures do you take in ensuring healthy balance in your life?*

7. *What factors do you think attribute to your episodes of prayerlessness?*

Chapter 10

THE ELEGANCE OF AN EAGLE WOMAN

Choosing To Soar High Above Your

Limilations

Chapter Preview

1. *You are a Leading Visionary who sees far and wide*

2. *You are a High Achiever who rides above mediocrity*

3. *You are an Innovator who feeds on what is fresh*

4. *You are a Promise Keeper who trusts after testing*

5. *You are an Empowerer who nurtures the next generation*

6. *You are a Master Strategist who uses the storms to lift you higher.*

7. *You are a Self-Rejuvenator who knows when to retreat and renew.*

OPENING REMARKS

"A strong woman is like an eagle; against the strong winds she soars." ~ **Gift Gugu Mona**

To fulfil your Purpose and Destiny, you must become an "**Eagle woman**" and adopt the qualities of an eagle in every area of your life, whether it be in leadership, business or family etc.

An "**Eagle woman**" is always ready to soar high and above in wide open spaces, of opportunities, beyond the norms to conquer and subdue hostile territories, overcome adverse circumstances.

"The eagle has no fear of adversity. We need to be like the eagle and have a fearless spirit of a conqueror." ~**Joyce Meyer**

As an "**Eagle woman**" your size symbolizes your awesome presence, strength, authority and power so that when you enter any space it is impossible to be ignored because of your largeness, significance, and relevance. Yet you remain grounded to reality and your humanity.

An "**Eagle woman**" inspires confidence, freedom, beauty, bravery, courage, honour, pride, determination and grace, having a great ability to inspire and push others to great heights of excellence and success.

"Eagles come in all shapes and sizes, but you will recognize them chiefly by their attitudes." ~ **E. F. Schumacher**

As an "**Eagle woman**" you are one who stretches limits refusing to settle for status quo and instead you reach higher and become more than you believe you are capable of.

Just like an Eagle has strong talons so too like an "**Eagle Woman**" you have the ability to hold on to and grasp tightly to that which is yours. You have strong feet which symbolizes your steadfast stable walk and life style of integrity that enables you to command respect and honour.

As an "**Eagle woman**" you never back down from a challenge, and you are not easily intimidated by that which you are pursuing to lay hold of no matter how big and impossible it looks.

Like an eagle, that builds its nest with thorns on the outside to protect its young ones from the enemy and then it puts soft twigs in the inner part of the nest to protect its young ones from injury, as an "**Eagle woman**" you should also ensure that the Visions you birth are protected from the enemy with the thorns you put around it, yet your Visions remain protected from the inside because of the protective measures systems and structures you put on the inside.

An "**Eagle woman**" is one who is committed to family, a good team player collaborating well to build great healthy families and to that extent she is a great contributor to building strong societies that ensures a strong nation.

By watching the way an eagle hunts its prey, how it nurtures and empowers its young, and how it commands the storm, it is clear that it is a divergent thinker and strategist. So, as an **Eagle woman**, you are also divergent in your thinking, a shrewd strategist who looks beyond the status quo to the multitude of possibilities.

1. YOU ARE A LEADING VISIONARY WHO SEES FAR AND WIDE

"Leadership is the capacity to translate Vision into reality." ~ **Warren Bennis**

An Eagle's eyesight is unique and extraordinary, designed for long distance focus and clarity, with an ability to detect its target over several miles away and to carefully plan its move to swiftly overwhelm it.

*"Eagles soar because they always focus on their goal." ~ **Unknown***

Like a dynamic Visionary leader, who sees far and beyond into the horizon, with a single-minded resolve, driven by Vision and Purpose. A strategic thinker who wisely weighs every decision and situation towards fulfilling her Vision and mission and to fiercely hold on that Vision and mission despite insurmountable odds.

An "**Eagle woman**" is one with a strong Vision for the future who is also focused and present with a powerful imagination positively able to visualize things easily and see future possibilities. You must be able to see big pictures and goals to see the whole process not just the single steps.

*"Live the Life of Your Dreams: Be brave enough to live the life of your dreams according to your Vision and Purpose instead of the expectations and opinions of others." ~ **Roy T. Bennett***

Your Vision needs to be sharp like that of an eagle so that you can see far and as to where you are going and as to how far your Purpose will impact, which means you will have a strong Vision for the future.

*"Only your Vision will define your limits." ~ **Unknown***

Like an eagle, your eyes have the ability to adjust according to the Vision you need to see, and as an "**Eagle woman**" your eye has the ability to see vividly and from a different and wider perspective and you are not narrow minded but able to see your goals from very far so that you start strategizing how to accomplish them.

"Vision is the art of seeing what is invisible to others." ~Jonathan Swift

This is because as like an eagle whose eyes are positioned in a way that they can have a peripheral Vision to see a wider circumference, you too are able to see all around you.

"Eagle women" are always open minded, innovative, energizers who recharge other people. They have clarity of Purpose; they have a strong powerful Vision for future and are strategic thinkers and planners and have the ability to hold their Vision and not be intimidated by obstacles.

Turn your Vision to reality by going the extra mile, being passionate, and action oriented and restless always soaring higher and higher.

"Eagle women" are never afraid of failure, or in other words they have come to terms with the fact that failure is inevitable, but one must get up and move beyond the failure.

They never give up, instead they take risks and transform them into opportunities, and they have the ability to share their Visions with other people articulately.

As a great Visionary, be accurate, always having the ability to predict and assess your future goals and plans, thus being a strategist, you have ability to see reality and you are not intimidated by size of your target, goals and what you need to lay hold of for your growth and empowerment.

Likewise, you will need to see the enemy of your Purpose approaching from very far, so that you are not caught off-guard or unaware.

Perhaps one of the greatest advantages of the eagles strong Vision is its ability to fight off enemies from its nest and its young, meaning that as an eagle woman your Visionary trait will always be one of your strongest strengths against the enemies of your dreams and Visions.

*"Haters like parrots talk much but cannot fly. Dreamers. Like eagles, say nothing but conquer the skies." ~ **Unknown**.*

2. YOU ARE A HIGH ACHIEVER WHO RIDES ABOVE MEDIOCRITY

*"I always knew I was gonna win, it was just a question of when and where." ~ **Unknown***

An eagle flies higher than any other bird symbolizing the trait of a high achiever, as an "Eagle woman" you will need to aim high in terms of excellence and be above average and above mediocre.

An eagle dwells and chooses to build its nest very high on the highest trees and on the highest mountain peaks, and refuses to dwell on the ground like chickens.

"You can't soar like an eagle when you hang out with chickens." ~
Unknown

Likewise, you will need to rise above the mundane and petty issues of everyday life and like an eagle you will rise up above and choose to dwell on the greater and higher things of life that empower and impact you for Destiny.

"May you soar on eagles' wings, high above the madness." ~
Jonathan Lockwood

Like a progressive woman who sets her mind on things above, aiming for audacious goals and surrounding herself with vibrant, like-minded global giants separating herself from anything base and retrogressive.

An eagle sometimes flies alone meaning that there are some seasons that you must separate yourself to focus on your Purpose and avoid distractions and too many voices. An Eagle prefers to fly alone, not because it is proud but because it is not afraid to soar high above the clouds where other birds will not dare fly.

Likewise, as an "**Eagle woman**" you are not afraid to go where other women fear to venture because you are a pioneer and a trail blazer, and hence the reason you must surround yourself with other eagle women of like mind.

"Don't be scared to fly alone, find a path that is your own." ~ *Anonymous*

A high flier aims for excellence, always optimistic, and goes for the very best, where there is air and unpolluted so that your mind is not cluttered. A high flier prefers high environment where there is less noise, so as to be able to think and meditate, where it is less crowded without mixed multitudes.

As a high flying "**Eagle woman**" you have the ability to hold on and not lose hope, in your dreams and Visions.

"Until you spread your wings you will have no idea how far you can fly." ~ *Napoleon Bonaparte*

An eagle woman is a problem solver not a murmurer or complainer, she makes things happen and whenever she steps into a situation the game changes.

An eagle has very heavy wings, so it has a very smart flying skills adopting stress-free gliding so as to rest its wings and conserve its energy. Likewise, because as an "**Eagle woman**" you have heavy responsibilities you must adopt very smart work skills and stress-free toil including smart living so that you can also conserve your energy and manage your time wisely.

Eagles fly with such swiftness meaning that as an "**Eagle woman**" your actions are prompt and without procrastination and you make timely choices and decisions.

"My advice is to never do tomorrow what you can do today; procrastination is the thief of time." ~ **Charles Dickens**

The higher eagles fly, the less noise they make meaning that as an Eagle woman the higher you climb the success ladder the less you speak about it because your accomplishments and achievements clearly speaks for themselves and they go ahead of you and testify for you.

Daniel 6:3 – *"Then this Daniel distinguished himself above the governors and satraps, because an excellent spirit was in him; and the king gave thought to setting him over the whole realm."*

3. YOU ARE AN INNOVATOR WHO FEEDS ON WHAT IS FRESH

"Innovation is the ability to see change as an opportunity not a threat." ~ **Steve Jobs**

An eagle will never eat anything that is dead or rotten, it always chooses to eat that which is alive. So too an "**eagle woman**" has the eating habits of an eagle demonstrating that she is an innovator because she chooses to feed on new and fresh ideas, easily adopts to new ways of doing things, she is receptive to progressive changes and processes and new radical experiences.

*"Without change there is no innovation, creativity, or incentive for improvement. Those who initiate change will have a better opportunity to manage the change that is inevitable." ~ **William Pollard***

An "**eagle woman**" is an innovative leader who rejects the outdated and stale and instead she seeks and embraces new and fresh creative ideas, she is development oriented and is always on the cutting edge in her field and sphere.

*"Innovation is seeing what everybody has seen, and thinking what nobody has thought." ~ **Dr. Albert Brent Gregory***

"**Eagle women**" are those who also like an eagle, are innovative in their receptivity of new ideas, progress and change and they are on the cutting edge of what is going on around them. So, they choose to feed on things that are pure, true, holy, and clean without defiling yourself with gossip, false or negative reports. She does not feed on past failures or past pain and wounds but on things that are edifying, and empowering, she guards what she takes in. (Philippians 4:8)

*"You are what you eat." ~ **Unknown***

As an "**Eagle Woman**" you have an insatiable inherent curiosity that constantly motivates you to keep seeking and searching for new and innovative ways of doing things. An "**eagle woman**" infectious passion fuels the innovative fire within her and she eagerly shares that passion with others.

An "**eagle woman**" is one who walks in truth, so she passes the integrity test because she knows how to handle and respond to offenses, slander, betrayal etc. Like the way an eagle takes its enemy the snake and hits it constantly against a rock until it dies. So too, you should take the lies of the serpent and hit them against the words of truth until those lies are destroyed and cast out of your life.

"At the end of the day, I believe truth is strongest than any lie that's out there." ~Ray Nagin

The choice of an **"eagle woman"** to be a fresh feeder like an eagle whereby she only takes in and feeds on the pure as opposed to the polluted, the updated as opposed to the outdated reinforces her integrity, honesty and strong moral values, high standards, excellence and superior qualities.

*"You must feed your mind even as you feed your body, and to make your mind healthy, you must feed it nourishing, wholesome thoughts." ~ **Norman Vincent Peale.***

4.   YOU ARE A PROMISE KEEPER WHO TRUSTS AFTER TESTING

*"Test before you trust but once you trust never test." ~ **PadamHeda***

An eagle is a covenant keeper because it values and commits to its relationships, it is loyal, trustworthy and dependable to its life mate and to its young. So too is an **"eagle woman"** a covenant keeper because she is loyal, trustworthy, committed and dependable in all her relationships whether they be business, professional, social, romantic, family and spiritual etc. She is also committed and faithful to those who she is mentoring, coaching, and ushering to Destiny.

*"We have to understand that there cannot be relationships unless there is commitment, unless there is loyalty, unless there is love, patience and persistence." ~ **Cornel West***

However, an eagle will test its relationships before it can trust and once it trusts and connects with another eagle, that relationship is for life. This symbolizes your ability as an **"eagle woman"** to sieve and sift all your relationships in order to vet and test their value and relevance to your Purpose and Destiny before committing to those relationships.

An eagle stays with one partner for life demonstrating a fierce loyalty and commitment to its relationships. Likewise, you must identify those Destiny relationships in your life that are intended for life and remain loyal and committed and even those other Destiny relationships that are for a season, you must be loyal and committed for the full season you are in them.

Once an eagle is committed it has amazing staying power. Like a wise **"Eagle woman"** who examines and vets every partnership, associations and collaboration in her life whether business, professional, social, etc. to ensure its value and legitimacy in relation to the Destiny.

"The best relationship is not the one being shared in good times but rather the one which has the staying power through rough times."
~ Unknown

An eagle's marriage is monogamous because it has one mate for life demonstrating its ability to choose its mate wisely at the onset and to thereafter maintain a healthy and strong relationship. To handle any challenges and conflicts within that relationship wisely so as to keep it for life, clearly showing that an eagle has very special relationship skills.

In fact, a female eagle takes the male eagle through a very rigorous process to test his commitment and to demonstrate to her how serious he is about having a relationship with her.

During courtship, the female eagle invites a male eagle into the air after picking up a log from the ground, and dropping it from a certain height for the male eagle to catch it. Once the male catches it and brings it back, the female flies to an even higher altitude and drops an even bigger log in the same way. This is repeated until the female gets the assurance that the male has mastered the art of catching the logs no matter how heavy and no matter what height as a sign of his diligence and commitment.

A male and female eagle once they commit into a "Marriage" and produce eaglets they team up together to raise up their young's and they share their parenting responsibilities very admirably.

Likewise, as an **"Eagle woman"** you must be able to choose your spouse wisely from the very beginning using a clearly well thought out criteria based on your fundamental values, beliefs and deal breakers. Thereafter you must be able to have or develop special people and social skills as well as conflict management skills coupled with a selflessness and an ability to effectively team work with your spouse in sharing your roles and responsibilities.

*"On a team it is not the strength of the individual player but the strength of the unit and how they all function together." ~ **Bill Belichick***

It is therefore clear that an eagle is relationship oriented, loyal and committed, and monogamous life. An **"eagle woman"** should be, loyal in relationships, always test commitment, by testing the ability to endure, test staying power, long-term not seasonal, test the value of each relationship.

*"Patience will show you if the bond is real or not. It is only so long you can "hold it down" for somebody that consistently lets you down!" ~ **Unknown***

5. YOU ARE AN EMPOWERER WHO NURTURES THE NEXT GENERATION

"A Woman is the full circle. Within her is the power to create, nurture and transform." ~ **Diane Mariechild**

An eagle is an excellent nurturer of its young, it will feed and protect but when the time comes to wean off its young and release them into their own destinies it will do so radically and swiftly without getting emotionally blinded into holding them back from their Destiny.

"After the initial pain of releasing our children, there comes joy and peace both for them and us." ~ **Stormie Omartian**

Likewise, an "**eagle woman**" is a nurturing empowerer, someone who supports, nourishes, fosters, and encourages another over a period of time with training, teaching, developing, impacting and influencing. A nurturing, empowering woman places a lot of value on friendships and relationships and emphasizes on trust. They prefer to use structures and routines in their training so as to maintain consistency, discipline, reliability and commitment on herself and those she is nurturing and empowering.

"A mentor empowers a person to see a possible future, and believe it can be obtained." ~ **Shawn Hitchcock**

This speaks, to your ability as an "**Eagle woman**" to invest in the dreams and Visions of others, empowering people by mentoring coaching, and impacting wisdom and ushering them to their destinies.

Eagles have amazing training skills, when weaning their young from their nest to real life, and moulding them to command the skies. Likewise, as a good leading "**Eagle woman**" leads the way and shows the way, provoking and empowering the others in her nation to arise and conquer great heights and become leading voices in their generation.

When the time comes, an eagle begins to remove the soft feathers that cushion the nest of its young, so that the eagles begin to get uncomfortable because of the prickly thorns and the eagle then starts the "weaning exercise" of dropping the eagle out of the nest to force the eaglet to learn how to fly."

As an "**eagle woman**" you are an empowerer and nurturer whereby you invest in training and equipping others, as a good mentor, and coach who thrives in feeding and nurturing her assignees so as to strengthen them, giving them directions and instructions to enable them fly to their Destiny.

"Be the one who nurtures and builds. Be the one who has an understanding and a forgiving heart one who looks for the best in people. Leave people better than you found them." ~ Marvin J. Ashton

Likewise, as an "**eagle woman**" you must challenge those you are ushering to Destiny through tough love as you push them out of their comfort zone. You should be careful to avoid emotional ties that may hinder her from letting go of those you are nurturing and empowering because you must release them into their greatness at the right time without holding on to them emotionally.

An **eagle woman** knows that the thorns of life come to teach us the need to grow, so like an eagle, she pushes her assignees out of the "comfortable nest by allowing the thorn of life to prick them.

Nurturers are natural givers of themselves and as a result of pouring themselves out into those they are nurturing and empowering. They can sometimes become depleted, exhausted and drained and even begin to question their relevance and effectiveness.

Consequently, you must ensure to walk in self-awareness, self-acceptance, self-respect, and self-confidence. Even in the event of that you feel taken advantage of, or those you are nurturing fail to see your value and become unappreciative, you will know that you still are a relevant "**eagle woman**" making a significant impact in the lives of others.

*"I nurture myself so I can nurture others." ~ **Unknown***

Perhaps one of the most admirable hallmarks and trademarks of a "**Eagle Woman**" is your ability to not only take care of your own Purpose and Destiny, but to also have the selfless ability to nourish, foster and empower others in enabling them fulfil their own Purposes and destinies. Promoting and provoking them, supporting and strengthening them, without losing focus on your own. You are by nature a nurturer, mentor, a coach, and a preserver of destinies.

*"Remember that nurturing yourself is as important as nurturing others." ~ **Mary Anne Radmacher***

In addition, your ability to also nurture and feed and cultivate other relationships in your life that are necessary for your Destiny, is crucial. Your understanding that fulfilling your Purpose and Destiny will require healthy relationships.

However, it is important for you to identify and distinguish the people and relationships that you have been called and assigned to nurture and dedicate your time to, (lest you zealously dedicate yourself to those who are not assigned to you and deny that time and dedication to the ones that you are really called and assigned for). Not everybody in the world is your assignment, learn to identify your "people". Or rather learn to identify your Destiny people and relationships.

6. YOU ARE A MASTER STRATEGIST WHO USES THE STORMS TO LIFT YOU HIGHER

"It is in the stormiest skies that eagles find their true Calling." **Matshona Dhliwayo**

The Eagle is the only bird that does not run away from the storm. Instead, it senses, when a storm is brewing sets its wings fearlessly flies directly into the **"eye of the storm"**. It positions itself wisely so that the strong pressure of the storm shoots it powerfully upwards out of the storm higher and higher up the sun, and out of all the birds of the air. It is the only bird that can survive the most vicious storms.

"There is beauty and serenity in the eye of the storm." *~Jonathan Lockwood Huie*

Likewise, as an **Eagle woman**, your Destiny will be faced with many storms. You must have the ability to weather every one of those storms, by confronting and flying into the eye of your storm and allowing the strong currents of that storm to propel you and shoot you into your Destiny.

Your test is in the storm, and the storm is your test. Like an eagle you must confront your storms as opposed to denying them or trying to run because it is the forceful viciousness of the storm that will push you up and out of it into your blessings.

"The greater the storm, the brighter your rainbow." ~ **Unknown**

The seat of adversity is the same seat of your blessing. Instead of looking for an umbrella during your rainy storm, you should dance in the rain. And like an Eagle learn to use the negative energy of your storms to rise even higher.

*"When you come out of the storm, you won't be the same person that walked in." ~ **Haruki Murakami***

Like a bold and courageous **"Eagle woman"** who does not turn away from challenges and storms. Instead, she sets her mind on and resolves to confront those challenges and storms head on knowing that, it is the turbulence in the storms of life that will strengthen and propel her to soar beyond ordinary limitations to new heights and opportunities.

An eagle takes advantage of every storm that other birds fear. This is because of the ability to lock its wings in a fixed position during a storm to stop them flapping so as to conserve energy.

*"In the eye of the storm you remain in control." ~ **Unknown***

Likewise, you must learn to not only survive the storms of life but also thrive during your storms, no matter how paradoxical that may sound.

An eagle's ability to use the storm to lift it up; gives it an opportunity to glide and rest its wings. You must beware against fretting during your storms because it will wear you out, and instead confront your storms wisely and smartly.

An Eagle is always careful not to get its wings wet because they become too heavy to fly, so it always seeks to soar higher than the rain. So, beware of allowing past pain and woundedness and other "wet" emotions to make your heart heavy and thereby hinder you from going higher and fulfilling your Destiny. Instead, you must learn to rise above the rains which symbolizes things that come to entangle and wear you down.

Psalm.107:29 – *"He calms the storm, so that its waves are still."*

7. YOU ARE A SELF-REJUVENATOR WHO KNOWS WHEN TO RETREAT AND RENEW

"Safe Care is important, when you take time to replenish your spirit, it allows you to serve others from the overflow. You can't serve from an empty vessel." ~ **By Eleanor Brown**

An eagle knows when it is time to take stock of self, retreat, and self-analyse to rest and repair, replenish and revive itself.

Eagles never give up living, so whenever they begin to sense the weakness of age. It is believed that they embark on rigorous rituals of renewing their youth and strength by flying away to a high secluded place and lying on a rock, drawing strength from the warm rays of the sun, shedding of its old self and allowing new growth, and new grace.

"Rest when you are weary. Refresh and renew yourself, your body, your mind, then get back to work." ~ **Ralph Marston**

Rejuvenation is to make young again, and restore youthfulness, vigour and appearance and basically make flesh and new again, in an act or processes of renewing oneself.

"You are my hiding place and my shield; I hope in Your word." **Psalm 119:114**

As an **eagle woman** you must also have the ability to know when you need to rest and to detox yourself of all outdated and unnecessary content and old ways of doing things. To empty yourself of baggage like past pain and failure so that you can receive fresh revelation, a fresh energy, and a fresh insight.

Eagle women who practice self-renewing and rejuvenation are driven by their principles, because they are intentional about their choices and preferences. They don't rejuvenate and renew themselves for the sake of change, but because they desire to upgrade their standards of excellence and be on the cutting edge. They connect and network effectively in order to grow and learn from others because self-renewing women never stop learning. Yet they require times of solitude and quietness to recharge and introspect privately.

"Hardships often prepare ordinary people for an extraordinary Destiny." By C. S. Lewis

An eagle has the ability to endure whatever pain it must in breaking off its old beak and plucking out its old feather so as to allow new ones to grow, and likewise as an eagle woman you must be willing to endure the process of renewing and rebranding yourself whenever necessary in order to remain relevant and valuable for fulfilling your Destiny.

"Endure and persist; this pain will turn to good by and by." By Ovid

So, like a zealous **eagle woman**, you must discern the need to constantly shed off old habits, outdated ideas, strange burdens, and baggage that weighs you down in your journey to Destiny.

So, you must retreat to the rock that is higher than you, (namely Jesus Christ) and let the warmth of the sun (son of God) renew you and revive you by His grace and give you a new strength to finish your race and finish well.

Isiaiah.40:31 – *"But those who wait on the LORD Shall renew their strength; They shall mount up with wings like eagles, They shall run and not be weary, They shall walk and not faint."*

Destiny Questions to Ponder On

1. *Which of these eagle traits do you believe you possess and how have they helped you in your journey to Destiny?*

2. *Which of these eagle traits do you not possess and how would you go about possessing them?*

3. *In which order of priority would you put these traits starting with the most important to the least important?*

4. *Are there any negative aspects about an eagle character in your opinion, if so, which ones?*

5. *How have you ensured that you constantly feed on what is fresh or how have you avoided feeding on things that are not fresh?*

6. *What nurturing skills have you adopted with regard to your mentees or biological children and how effective have they been in empowering them?*

7. *Do you believe that you have learnt how to master the storms in your life so far or is there any storm that you did not master and what were the consequences?*

WORDS HAVE POWER

Relevant Quotes and Scripture Meditations

for Your Making and Shaping

Inspirational Quotes and Scriptures about the Woman of Destiny

"*Strong women not only feel pain, they accept it, they learn from it and fight through it. They turn their wounds into wisdom. They may fall, but they always get back up, dust off, and fight like they have never fought before.*" By **Unknown**

"*A woman who is at rest with herself has nothing to prove to others, she embraces her strengths & cheers others on with a pure heart. Her light shines brightly; her words are seasoned with kindness, goodness & grace. She is peaceful & edifies others as she is secure in her Heavenly Father.*" By **Hanna Bryant**

"*God has a purpose for your pain, a reason for your struggle and a reward for your faithfulness. Trust Him and don't give.*" By **Dave Willis**

"*She may be quiet, but she's a warrior and her prayers can move mountains.*" **Unknown**

"*She is not broken anymore, she is stronger, wiser and more beautiful than before, because God took her broken pieces and made her new again.*" By **Unknown**

"*Though my soul may set in darkness, it will rise in perfect light; I have loved the stars too fondly to be fearful of the night.*" By **Sarah Williams**

"*In the end, she became more than she was expected. She became the journey, and like all journeys, she did not end, she just simply changed directions and kept going.*" By **R.M. Drake**

"*Mirror! Mirror! on the wall, I'll always get up after I fall. And whether I run, walk or have to crawl, I'll set my goals and achieve them all.*" By **Brie Edison**

"I am a strong woman because a strong woman raised me." By **Unknown**

"We all have an unsuspected reserve of strength inside that emerges when life puts us to test." By **Isabel Allende**

"Keep your head up. God gives his hardest battles to his strongest soldiers." By **Unknown**

"If you feel like you are losing everything, remember that trees lose their leaves every year and they still stand tall and wait for better days to come." By **Unknown**

"Strength grows in the moments when you think you can't go on, but you keep going anyway." By **Unknown**

"Some women are lost in the fire. Some women are built from it." By **Michelle K**

"I know you're tired, you're fed up, you're so close to breaking, but there is strength within you even when you feel weak. Keep fighting. By **Unknown**

"Strength doesn't come from what you can do. It comes from overcoming the things you once thought you couldn't. By **Rikki Rogers**

"It's actually pretty simple. Either you do it, or you don't." By **Unknown**

"She believed she could, so she did." By **R.S. Grey**

"I'm proud of the woman I am because I went through one hell of a time becoming her." By **Unknown**

"The circles of women in our lives weave invisible nets of love that carry us when we are weak, and they sing with us when we are strong." By **Sark**

"Behind every successful woman is a tribe of other successful women, who have her back." By **Kimberly**

"Women should empower each other, instead of being so hateful and envious of one another." By **Unknown**

"A successful woman is one who can build a firm foundation with the bricks others have thrown to her." By **Unknown**

"It took me quite a long time to develop a voice, and now that I have it I am not going to be silent." By **Madeleine Albright**

"She overcomes everything that was meant to destroy her." By **Sylvester McNutt III**

"When women support each other, incredible things happen." By **Viola Davis**

"Each time a woman stands up for herself, she stands up for all women." By **Maya Angelou**

"A woman is unstoppable after she realizes she deserves better." By **Yene D.**

"I am obsessed with seeing women encourage, support, and empower other women. It's my favorite, we need more of it." By **Unknown**

"I would like to be known as an intelligent woman, a courageous woman, a loving woman, a woman who teaches by being." By **Maya Angelou**

"*Here's to strong women, may we know them, may we be them, may we raise them.*" By **Unknown**

"*She never seemed shattered; to me she was the breathtaking mosaic of the battles she won.*" By **Unknown**

"*A strong woman, looks a challenge in the eye, and gives it a wink.*" By **Gina Carey**

"*Never underestimate the power of a kind woman. Kindness is a choice that comes from incredible strength.*" By **Unknown**

"*She surrounds herself with women she can grow with.*" By **Unknown**

"*When a woman is loved correctly, she becomes ten times, the woman she was before.*" By **Unknown**

"*A woman unaffected by insult has made her enemies absolutely powerless.*" By **Entity**

"*A strong woman in her essence is a gift to the world.*" By **Unknown**

"*I want every girl to know that her voice can change the world.*" By **Malala Yousafzai**

"*Women who compliment other women genuinely are a whole different breed. Real Queens*" By **Unknown**

"*Nothing is more impressive than a woman who is secure in the unique way God made her.*" By **Rhonda Kulczyk**

"*Empowered women empower women.*" By **Unknown**

"*A foolish woman keeps talking, a wise woman understands the power of her words as well as her silence.*" By **Unknown**

"And one day she discovered, that she was fierce, and strong, and full of fire, and that not even she could hold herself back, because her passion burned brighter than her fears." By **Mark Anthony**

"We need women who are so strong, they can be gentle, so educated they can be humble, so fierce they can be compassionate, so passionate they can be rational, and so disciplined they can be free." By **Kavita N. Ramdas**

"A strong woman is a woman determined to do something others are determined not to be done." By **Marge Piercy**

"Be strong enough to let go, and wise enough to wait for what you deserve." By **Unknown**

"Strong women lift each other up." By **Unknown**

"A woman is like a tea bag; you never know how strong it is until it is in hot water." By **Eleanor Roosevelt**

"A strong woman is one, who feels deeply and loves fiercely, her tears flow just as abundantly as her laughter. A strong woman is both soft and powerful, she is both practical and spiritual, a strong woman in her essence is a gift to the world." By **Unknown**

"Strong women wear their pain like stilettos, no matter how much it hurts, all you see is the beauty of it. By **Harriet Morgan**

"Success isn't about how much money you make, it's about the difference you make in people's lives." By **Michelle Obama**

"To attract money, you must focus on wealth. It is impossible, to bring more money into your life, when you are noticing you don't have enough because that means you are thinking thoughts that you don't have enough." By **Rhonda Byrne**

"You can only become truly accomplished at something you love. Don't make money your goal. Instead pursue the things you love doing and then do them so well that people can't take their eyes off you." By **Maya Angelou**

"Here's to financially independent Women, may we know them, may we be them, may we raise them." By **Unknown**

"People, who have drawn wealth into their lives, used the secret consciously or unconsciously, they think thoughts of abundance of wealth, and they don't allow any contradictory to take roots in their minds." By **Rhonda Byrne**

"Save your money and one day your money will save you." By **Unknown**

"Nearly every glamorous, wealthy, successful career woman, you might envy now, started out as some kind of schlep. By **Helen Gurley Brown**

"A business career for a woman, and her needs for a woman's life, as wife and mother, are not enemies at all, unless we make them so. But maybe the closest and most co-operative friends and supporters of each other." By **Hortense Oldum**

"Leadership is about making others better as a result of your presence and making sure that impact lasts in your absence." By **Sheryl Sandberg**

"Women need to shift from thinking I'm not ready to do that to I'll learn by doing it." By **Sheryl Sandberg**

"If your actions create a legacy that inspires others to dream more, learn more, do more and become more, then, you are an excellent leader." By **Dolly Parton**

"*I just want women to always feel in control, because we are capable, we're so capable.*" By **Nicki Minaj**

"*A leader takes people where they want to go. A great leader takes people where they don't necessarily want to go, but ought to be.*" By **Rosalynn Carter**

"*Because I am a woman, I must make unusual effort to succeed. If I fail, no one will say, 'She doesn't have what it takes.' They will say, women don't have what it takes.*" By **Unknown**

"*Our deepest fear is not that we are inadequate. Our deepest fear is that we are powerful beyond measure.*" By **Marianne Williamson**

"*Leadership is hard to define and good leadership even harder. But if you can get people to follow you to the end of the earth, you are a great leader.*" By **Indra Nooyi**

"*People respond well to those that are sure of what they want.*" By **Anna Wintour**

"*No power on earth compares to a mother's tender prayer.*" By **Edwin Arnold**

"*I remember my mother's prayer and they have always followed me. They have clung to me all my life.*" By **Abraham Lincoln**

"*The battle for our children's lives is waged on our knees.*" By **Stormie Omartian**

"*Prayer warrior mothers cover their kids with God's blessings and protection.*" By **Marla Alupoaicei**

"*Every mother's prayer; guide her to a place where she'll be safe.*" By **Carole Bayer Sager**

"The bond between mothers and their children is one defined by love. As a mother's prayer for her children are unending, so are the wisdom, grace and strength they provide for their children." By **President George W. Bush**

"God does hear and answer prayers. . . From childhood, at my mother's knee where I first learned to pray . . . I know without question that it is possible for men and women to reach out in humility and prayer and tap that Unseen Power." ~**Ezra Taft Benson**

"During all those years of struggle and heartache, my mother never worried. She took all her troubles to God in prayer." ~**Dale Carnegie**

"My mother knew when to listen and when to pray and when to help. I wonder how many people knew the compassion [my mother] held for them and how hard, in the privacy of her God Box, she prayed for them and their struggles." ~**Mary Lou Quinlan**

"To this day, even though I am grown and have two children of my own, whenever I travel somewhere distant or am undertaking a major project, my mother will sit me down, lay hands on me, and say a prayer of blessing." ~**Francisco J. García** Jr.

"From the time of my earliest memories, she impressed upon me one rule above all others: when I woke from sleep, my first duty was to pray to God for spiritual nourishment and blessings . . . my mother would never relent . . . She planted in me, and tended in my early life, a profound love and fear of God." ~**Sadhu Sundar Singh**

<u>Bible Wisdom About The Woman Of Destiny</u>

Proverbs 31:30; "Charm is deceitful and beauty is passing, But a woman who fears the LORD, she shall be praised."

Psalm 46:5 "God is in the midst of her, she shall not be moved; God shall help her, just at the break of dawn."

Proverbs 31:16-17 "She considers a field and buys it; from her profits she plants a vineyard. She girds herself with strength, and strengthens her arms."

1 Corinthians 15:10 "But by the grace of God I am what I am, and His grace toward me was not in vain; but I labored more abundantly than they all, yet not I, but the grace of God *which was* with me."

Proverbs 31:20-21 "She extends her hand to the poor, Yes, she reaches out her hands to the needy. She is not afraid of snow for her household, For all her household *is* clothed with scarlet."

Psalm 139:14 "I will praise You, for I am fearfully and wonderfully made; Marvellous are Your works, And that my soul knows very well."

1 Corinthians 11:12 "For as woman came from man, even so man also comes through woman; but all things are from God."

1 Peter 3:3-4 "Do not let your adornment be merely outward—arranging the hair, wearing gold, or putting on fine apparel—rather let it be the hidden person of the heart, with the incorruptible beauty of a gentle and quiet spirit, which is very precious in the sight of God."

1 Timothy 3:11 "Likewise, their wives must be reverent, not slanderers, temperate, faithful in all things."

Luke 1:45 "Blessed is she who believed that there will be a fulfilment of those things which were told her from the Lord."

Proverbs.31:20 "She extends her hand to the poor, Yes, she reaches out her hands to the needy."

Proverbs 11:16 "A gracious woman retains honor, But ruthless *men* retain riches."

Proverbs 31:25 "Strength and honor *are* her clothing; She shall rejoice in time to come."

Proverbs 3:15 "She *is* more precious than rubies, And all the things you may desire cannot compare with her."

Proverbs 31:26 "She opens her mouth with wisdom, And on her tongue *is* the law of kindness."

Proverbs. 14:1 "The wise woman builds her house, But the foolish pulls it down with her hands.

Proverbs. 19:13 "A foolish son is the ruin of his father, And the contentions of a wife are a continual dripping."

Proverbs. 21:9 "Better to dwell in a corner of a housetop, Than in a house shared with a contentious woman."

Proverbs. 31: 17-18 "She girds herself with strength, And strengthens her arms. She perceives that her merchandise is good, And her lamp does not go out by night."

Proverbs.21:19 "Better to dwell in the wilderness, Than with a contentious and angry woman."

Proverbs. 31: 16 "She considers a field and buys it; From her profits she plants a vineyard."

Proverbs.12:4 "An excellent wife is the crown of her husband, But she who causes shame is like rottenness in his bones."

Proverbs. 31:19 "She stretches out her hands to the distaff, And her hand holds the spindle.

Proverbs. 31:10-12 "Who can find a virtuous wife? For her worth is far above rubies. The heart of her husband safely trusts her; So he will have no lack of gain. She does him good and not evil All the days of her life."

Proverbs. 31:13-15 "She seeks wool and flax, And willingly works with her hands. She is like the merchant ships, She brings her food from afar. She also rises while it is yet night, And provides food for her household, And a portion for her maidservants."

Proverbs.31:26 "She opens her mouth with wisdom, And on her tongue is the law of kindness."

Ephesians.5:22-23 "Wives, submit to your own husbands, as to the Lord. For the husband is head of the wife, as also Christ is head of the church; and He is the Savior of the body."

1st Peter. 3:1-2 "Wives, likewise, be submissive to your own husbands, that even if some do not obey the word, they, without a word, may be won by the conduct of their wives, when they observe your chaste conduct accompanied by fear."

Titus. 2:3-5 "The older women likewise, that they be reverent in behaviour, not slanderers, not given to much wine, teachers of good things— that they admonish the young women to love their husbands, to love their children to be discreet, chaste, homemakers, good, obedient to their own husbands, that the word of God may not be blasphemed."

1st **Tim. 2:9-10** "In like manner also, that the women adorn themselves in modest apparel, with propriety and moderation, not with braided hair or gold or pearls or costly clothing, but, which is proper for women professing godliness, with good works."

1st **Cor. 11:3** "But I want you to know that the head of every man is Christ, the head of woman is man, and the head of Christ is God."

1st **Tim.5:14** "Therefore I desire that the younger widows marry, bear children, manage the house, give no opportunity to the adversary to speak reproachfully."

Col.3:18-19 "Wives, submit to your own husbands, as is fitting in the Lord. Husbands, love your wives and do not be bitter toward them."

Proverbs.31:27 "She watches over the ways of her household, And does not eat the bread of idleness."

2nd **Tim.1:5** "when I call to remembrance the genuine faith that is in you, which dwelt first in your grandmother Lois and your mother Eunice, and I am persuaded is in you also."

Proverbs.31:28 "Her children rise up and call her blessed; Her husband also, and he praises her."

Proverbs.31:25 "Strength and honour are her clothing; She shall rejoice in time to come."

Proverbs 18:22 "He who finds a wife finds a good thing, And obtains favour from the LORD."

Proverbs.23:22 "Listen to your father who begot you, And do not despise your mother when she is old."

Proverbs.4:6 "Do not forsake her, and she will preserve you; Love her, and she will keep you."

Proverbs.11:22 "As a ring of gold in a swine's snout, so is a lovely woman who lacks discretion."

Proverbs.31:21 "She is not afraid of snow for her household, For all her household is clothed with scarlet."

BIBLIOGRAPHY

The Bible

Jakes, T.D.2002.*God's Leading Lady: Out of the Shadows and into the Light*. Berkley.

Sandberg, Sheryl & Scovell, Nell.2013.*Lean In: Women, Work, and the Will to Lead*. Alfred A. Knopf.

Stigel, V. Herta.2011.*The Mountain Within: Leadership Lessons and Inspiration for Your Climb to the Top*. McGraw-Hill Eductaion.

Scott, Janny.2011.*A Singular Woman: The Untold Story of Barack Obama's Mother*. Riverhead Books.

Meyer, Joyce.2010.*Eat the Cookie… Buy the Shoes: Giving Yourself Permission to Lighten Up*. FaithWords.

Karssen, Gien.1974.*Her Name is Woman*. NavPress Publishing Group.

Live By Faith by Rev. Teresa Wairimu

Yancey, Philip.2002.*Where Is God When It Hurts?* Zondervan.

Shellenberger, Susie & Gowler, Kathy.2007.*What Your Daughter Isn't Telling You: Expert Insight Into the World of Teen Girls*. Bethany House Publishers.

Boundaries by Pastor Sammy Hinn

Covey, R. Stephen.2004.*The 7 Habits of Highly Effective People: Powerful Lessons in Personal Change*. Free Press.

Dr. D. W. Ekstrand, 2012. The Influence Parents have on their Children. Accessed on 28th July, 2020 http://www.thetransformedsoul.com/additional-studies

Sasha, 2016: The influence of a good teacher can never be erased. Accessed on 28th July, 2020 https://mirrorgirlblog.wordpress.com/2016/09/17/

Leslie Becker-Phelps, PHD, 2005; Ways your Friends Influence your Future. Accessed on https://blogs.webmd.com/relationships/20160928

Brandon Thomas, 2008: Does past experience affect what we see or what we do? accessed on 29th July, 2020 https://www.researchgate.net/post/Does_past_experience

Art Markman, Ph.D. 2011: Your View of the Future Is Shaped by the Past. Accessed on 29th July, 2020 https://www.psychologytoday.com/us/blog/ulterior-motives/201108

Orit E. Tykocinski and Andreas Ortmann. 2011: The Lingering Effects of Our Past Experiences: The Sunk-Cost Fallacy and the Inaction-Inertia Effect. Accessed on 29th July, 2020 http://portal.idc.ac.il/he/schools/psychology/

Claire Newton. 2020: Destiny: Action or Accident? Accessed on 29th July 2020 http://www.clairenewton.co.za/my-articles/destiny-action-or-accident.html

Sandra Dawes.2014. Following your inner voice. Accessed on 29th July, 2020 https://embraceurdestiny.com/2014/01/29/following-your-inner-voice/

Kenneth Copeland, 2018. Ways to Know If You're Hearing God's Voice. Accessed on 29th July,2020 https://blog.kcm.org/4-ways-know-youre-hearing-gods-voice/

Pincott Jena E, 2019. Silencing Your Inner Critic, accessed on 29th July, 2020 https://www.psychologytoday.com/us/articles/2019 3/silencing-your-inner-critic

Bonnie Badenoch, Ph.D. 2010. Critical Inner Voice. Accessed on 29th July, 2020 https://www.psychalive.org/critical-inner-voice/

Bibliography